ONE WOMAN'S
WORLD WAR II

ONE WOMAN'S
WORLD WAR II

Violet A. Kochendoerfer

THE UNIVERSITY PRESS OF KENTUCKY

Copyright © 1994 by The University Press of Kentucky

Scholarly publisher for the Commonwealth,
serving Bellarmine College, Berea College, Centre
College of Kentucky, Eastern Kentucky University,
The Filson Club, Georgetown College, Kentucky
Historical Society, Kentucky State University,
Morehead State University, Murray State University,
Northern Kentucky University, Transylvania University,
University of Kentucky, University of Louisville,
and Western Kentucky University.

Editorial and Sales Offices: Lexington, Kentucky 40508-4008

Library of Congress Cataloging-in-Publication Data

Kochendoerfer, Violet A.
  One woman's World War II / Violet A. Kochendoerfer.
    p.   cm.
  ISBN 0-8131-1866-2 (alk. paper)
  1. Kochendoerfer, Violet A., 1912–   . 2. World War, 1939–1945—
Personal narratives, American. 3. United States. Army. Women's
Auxiliary Army Corps—Biography. 4. American National Red Cross—
Biography. I. Title. II. Title: One woman's World War 2.
III. Title: One woman's World War Two.
D811.5.K5944 1994
940.54'771'092--dc20   93-38919
[B]

This book is printed on acid-free recycled paper meeting
the requirements of the American National Standard
for Permanence of Paper for Printed Library Materials.
♾

Contents

Introduction

My three and a half years in the War now seems a small but poignant episode of my varied life. It began with "sweating out" buzz bombs in London and watching the C-47s of the 315th Troop Carrier Group take off with paratroopers on D-Day. On the Continent, I was with 82d Airborne when that "All-American Division" made the last bridgehead of the war—crossing the Elbe, meeting the Russians, and liberating a concentration camp as the main German army surrendered to our General James Gavin.

I was then wearing the uniform of the American Red Cross, which had replaced my earlier one in the Women's Army Auxiliary Corps. At five feet eight inches tall I proudly wore both uniforms, just as I'd worn well-designed clothes made by my seamstress mother through high school days in Winona, Minnesota.

I grew up in a lower-middle-class family in the 1920s and, as the Great Depression of the 1930s followed, had no thought of going to college. Few of my friends were headed that way. The goal of most girls was to find a husband and raise a family. That wasn't my choice; I envisioned myself in the business world. My folks couldn't afford college; nor was there a student loan fund, and anyway, I was part of a family who paid cash for things. If we didn't have the money, we did without.

My record as salutatorian of my class in high school did earn me a good position as secretary to the president of Winona State Teachers College, where I enjoyed the academic atmosphere. I spent a lot of my spare time at the YWCA, and even more important to my later life than playing on a champion basketball team there was my friendship with a YW Secretary, who finally convinced me that I had to go to college.

Along with that decision I made another. I'd always envied students who went away to college and then could go home for the holidays; I would leave home so I could do just that. I had relatives in Portland and began writing to colleges in Oregon; and when a WSTC professor heard this, he said, "If you're going to Oregon, you must go to Reed!" I didn't know then what I do now, that this small liberal arts college has an enviable reputation as a pioneer in progressive education, founded on the principle of teaching students to think for themselves. Even today, in educational circles, if they hear you went to Reed College, you're immediately labeled a "brain."

At any rate, Reed said that with the $1,800 I'd saved, plus work on campus, I could get by financially—and I did, for two years. Then my money ran out, and I became a college employee instead of a student. I was assistant to Easton Rothwell, the new dean of men, who became a lifelong friend and mentor. Although he later was director of the Hoover War Library at Standford, and president of Mills College in California—and associated with important people around the world—as one of his many assistants I was always to feel special in his large circle of friends.

After less than two years Easton took a leave of absence for a special assignment in the State Department. He was temporarily replaced by a man who was everything I couldn't abide in the way of values and approach to students. When he insisted that the offices be redecorated and old furniture replaced, I wanted to tell him that students came in to see the man *behind* the desk. Before he could fire me, I resigned and did something I had always said I'd never do: I went to work for the government and was the first employee of the new Office of Price Administration in the state of Oregon.

I took the job of junior stenographer at $1,440 a year with the stipulation that I could have any position I could handle as the office developed. When a state director was hired, I became his secretary. As the agency grew out of its two rooms to occupy two floors of the Bedell Building, I moved on up to be in charge of much of the personnel hiring. When the salary in that position reached a CAF-14 ($7,000-$8,000), the regional office wanted a man to fill it. Our state director said, "We have every confidence in Miss Kochendoerfer and want her in that capacity." He was told, "If you can't find a man in Portland, we'll send you one from San Francisco."

I'd had my own secretary. The new man put a typewriter back on my desk, and once again I resigned. That third resignation set the tenor for future years. I had come to realize that one lifetime is too short even to begin to tap all possibilities. If I wasn't happy or excited about what I was doing, staying put was too high a price to pay for security. So, almost against my better judgment, I joined the Women's Army Auxiliary Corps, which had been established by act of Congress on May 14, 1942, to introduce women into the military.

The first eight months I spent in the United States with the Women's Army Auxiliary Corps. The year was 1943. I was twenty-six years old. When I elected not to enlist in the Women's Army Corps, I was attracted to the American Red Cross because it opened the possibility of foreign service and travel when these were available only to a privileged few. I was with the ARC in the European Theater of Operations (ETO) from D-Day well into the occupation of Germany.

It was history's perhaps most memorable war, monumental in its complete and utter defeat of the war machines of the Axis powers. Historic also was the military's inclusion of women in supporting roles. Established in 1942, the Women's Army Auxiliary Corps and its successor, the Women's Army Corps, pioneered in the process of freeing men for combat by providing skilled technical services. But the organization became vulnerable to stresses caused by the rapid buildup of the war—false starts, imperfect planning and implementation, masculine hostility, skepticism, and slander. Colonel Oveta Culp Hobby, its director, has said (in the 1953 government series, *U.S. Army in World War II: The Women's Army Corps*): "No new agency requiring social change has escaped a similar baptism. I feel now that nothing we might have done could have avoided it." Major General Orlando Ward, Chief of Military History, concluded his Foreword to

the same volume: "The WAC did not always understand the
Army—its needs and its customs and traditions, its organization and necessary chain of command. The Army did not
always understand the WAC—its needs and temperament,
and the many other things that man, being the son of woman, should have known but did not, much to his continued
embarrassment."

Although we tend to think of the Red Cross in terms of disaster relief, it was actually born on the battle scene. The International Red Cross was formed at the Geneva Convention in
1864 to provide for the formation of a volunteer civilian organization to give aid to the wounded in wartime and provide con-
ditions of neutrality not only for wartime wounded but also for
volunteers and their materials and equipment. The United
States did not ratify the convention until 1881, after relentless
pursuit by Clara Barton, who is known as the founder of the
American Red Cross. By an 1882 proclamation, it became
unique in our organization history. Under authority from a
later Congressional charter in 1905 the present-day American
Red Cross was charged with specific responsibilities—using
primarily volunteer personnel to provide services to members of the armed forces, disaster prevention and relief, and
other government-requested assistance.

In World War I, American Red Cross supplied medical personnel, ambulance units, and base hospitals. In World War II
these duties were largely replaced with hospital service, emergency home leave services, blood programs, and personal services to the troops in the form of cigarettes, magazines, writing paper, sheets, and towels. When recreation was added to
its special responsibilities to help in maintaining troop morale,
it turned out to be the largest project in the organization's history. The American Red Cross provided some 75 rest homes
for combat fliers, 400 service clubs in leave areas, 500 on-post
clubs plus "clubmobile" service on the line in the ETO, 190
canteens at remote airstrips, and 300 mobile canteens in the
South Pacific. Locations and kinds of services were chosen
entirely by the military, which could request facilities for officers, enlisted men, or mixed groups. With troops moving as

the war progressed, the opening and closing of facilities constantly changed the scene in which we worked. Once assigned, we were often on our own in working with the military. I served as director of base clubs in England, France, and Germany and in a leave center in Bavaria. As paid Red Cross personnel, we hired and paid indigenous staff.

As with the WAAC, rumors proliferated. It was charged that Red Cross girls sold the cigarettes and other items purchased with funds contributed at home. Red Cross girls were also accused of questionable morals and of snobbery. Efforts were made to track down the rumors of sales, but without success. Although some may have occurred, it was felt that such stories were largely initiated by unhappy GIs with ulterior motives. Morals charges were also greatly exaggerated; our relationships with men were in general naive by today's standards. From a background where I had learned that men who were "brung up right" didn't proposition women, I quickly learned to pigeonhole servicemen by the "lines" I was to hear over and over again. I picked my dates accordingly. That Red Cross girls (though women, we were always called "girls") associated chiefly with officers was a result of our assimilated military rank of captain, intended for our protection in case of capture. Our private lives in combat areas were set by the same standards as those of army nurses, who were commissioned officers and, as such, were not to fraternize with enlisted men. We didn't always hold to this rule, but it left us vulnerable to charges of snobbishness.

My story is told in part in slightly edited excerpts from what I wrote home to family and friends. I was so busy much of the time that I didn't write often, but I did keep journals. When I did write (often taking portions verbatim from my journals), I made typed carbon copies on Red Cross onionskin paper and sent them, together with a personal note, to my parents, my sister's family, and two friends. My mother kept an entire file of the original copies. Some of these newsletters, such as the "issues" of my WAAC News and the Ludwigslust story with the 82d Airborne, have been included largely as written; others are abbreviated. Much information that is not in letter form is based on additional correspondence that is too voluminous to include but today offers a record of events, circumstances, and feelings as I experienced them.

It is my hope that my story will open a window to the past. World War II, now in its half-century anniversary, is the stuff of history, yet there are relatively few memoirs of this period written by women. Although I was not among the high and mighty, I did participate in historic moments with important military units and officers. This is my story, one woman's World War II.

PART I
My Two Uniforms

1 Basic Training in the WAAC

I didn't join the Women's Army Auxiliary Corps to help my country's war effort. I did it in selfish rebellion when my rise in the business world was thwarted because I was a woman. Once I had passed the physical and aptitude tests and had been fingerprinted, however, my angry feelings subsided. I was off on a new adventure. I found I loved being stopped on the street by envious or questioning friends and associates, and interviewed by newspaper reporters. I had promised family and friends to share the experience, so I took my portable typewriter along to produce my "WAAC News."

WAAC News No. 1.
Portland, Oregon, Monday, January 11, 1943

Got my sailing orders last Friday. I report to Fort Des Moines for basic training. Guess I'll be missed at the office from all everyone says, "How will we get along without you?" To be honest, it feels good to be leaving all the responsibility behind, but I wonder how I'll like the military discipline! I'm hoping I can get into officer training right after basic. That may be optimistic, but it doesn't hurt to hope.

I'm having an awful time passing up January sales, especially the hats. Good feeling, though, in knowing I won't be needing a thing. They furnish everything—bras, girdles, socks, robes, bedroom slippers, shoes. That's good, for I'll be making only $50 a month.

You're bound to have lots of questions. Let me start by answering some. From one brochure:

1. What Is the Women's Army Auxiliary Corps? It is a corps of women in military uniform and under military discipline, organized for noncombatant service with the Army. It is the only

women's organization, exclusive of the Army Nurse Corps, authorized to serve with the Army.

2. How Is It Set Up? Organization will be along military lines. There will be a Director, Assistant Director, Officers and Auxiliaries. Auxiliaries are the equivalent of the enlisted men in the Army.

3. Who Can Join? An applicant must . . . be a woman citizen of the United States . . . be between her 21st and 45th birthdays . . . have an excellent character . . . pass an intelligence test . . . submit satisfactory proof of birth date and citizenship . . . qualify according to height and weight chart . . . present character references from responsible business or professional people in her community (not relatives) who are personally acquainted with the applicant's ability. Service wives are eligible. Married women with children under 14 are ineligible.

4. What Kind of Work Will I Do? . . . You will at once be given the basic training, which lasts four weeks and consists of Army orientation, drill, physical training, and such subjects as mess management, map reading and military sanitation. At the completion of this training, you will be given a series of aptitude tests to determine what type of work you will be best fitted for in your service with the Army. [At present] schools include Administration, Motor Transport, Bakers and Cooks, Communications, and Radio. As the Corps expands, other types of specialist training will be added. The discipline as well as the training of the WAAC is along military lines. You will be governed by the Code of Conduct established in WAAC Regulations.

5. Can I Become an Officer? Every applicant accepted will be enrolled as an Auxiliary. As the Corps expands, each member will have an equal opportunity to be selected for Officers Training School on the basis of all-around performance and ability.

6. How Long Is the Enrollment? The term of service is for the duration of the war and for not more than six months thereafter. The Secretary of War may discharge any member for cause, disability, or for the convenience of the Government. Members upon application may be given an honorable discharge in case of personal reasons of an emergency nature, and each case will be decided on its individual merit.

7. Will I Wear a Uniform? Every member of the Women's Army Auxiliary Corps will wear the appropriate uniforms, insignia, and accessories supplied by the Government.

8. How Much Furlough Time Do I Get? A member is entitled to thirty days' leave, or furlough, per year.

9. What Will I Be Paid? 1st Leader $138; Technical Leader $114; Staff Leader $96; Leader $78; Junior Leader $66; Auxiliary 1st Class $54; Auxiliary $50.

Sounds as though I'll have to get used to doing everything "the Army way!" At the office I wrote my own letter of recommendation for my boss's signature. The draft copy I gave him was returned with the notation in pen, "Okay. Couldn't have done better myself!" Now that I look at my own description of myself, I begin to wonder just how this will fit in the command situation of the Army! I'll be a number now, and wonder how Auxiliary A-906-242 will look in her uniform!

WAAC News No. 2
Fort Des Moines, Iowa, Wednesday, January 28, 1943
We just had our first round of shots, and they've given us an hour off to take it easy—the first whole hour we've had to ourselves since we came. Several fainted in line just thinking of those needles. The docs were cagey. . . . just as we went through a door there was someone on both sides all posted to plunge that needle in! Just thinking about it was almost worse than the shots themselves. With all of that, we're loving every minute of it. . . .

Just learned that this really was a fort built about 1840 to protect the Whites from the Indians. In the early nineteen hundreds it became the largest cavalry post in the U.S.

The Food is OK and the service good, since we do it ourselves. The aluminum mess tray is all divided up in geometric shapes. Those behind the counter just plop the food on in the right spot. We drink coffee out of sugar bowls without handles, and have to learn how to use them with one hand. We drink milk right out of the bottle. If you want water, you drink the milk first, and then use the bottle for water. The only gripe I have is that we have to rush through everything, including meals.

We got our first uniform! For the cold weather we were issued EM [enlisted men's] coats. They just threw them at us over the counter. Most are oversized and come down to our ankles. You'll die at pics of us we took with me in spike heels poking out from under those crazy long coats, and the crazy little knit caps with a bill. By "us" I mean Isabel (Izzie) a short, pudgy phys. ed. teacher from Portland and tall, attractive Liz, two swell Portlanders I met on the train. We're going to stick together as long as we can.

A little Handbook we just got, in answer to the question "Why are you here?" said:

The purpose of the Corps is to make available the knowledge, skill, and special training of the women of our Nation for the war effort.

You are part of that Corps now. We know you can do a good job, but the Army has to teach you a few things first. That's why you are here at the Fort Des Moines Training Center. You will probably have to do many things you never did before, but a good soldier adjusts herself quickly to military life.

While you're here, you'll learn how to salute, how to march, how to handle a gas mask, how to make a bed the Army way, and how to look like a soldier. Those of you with specialties will be encouraged, others will learn specialties. There are facilities here to train you. The Post has been dressed up to make you comfortable. Sure, there will be some things lacking and some things you don't like about it, but all these things will come out all right.

I don't particularly like their psychology—treating us like children—but I suppose that's the Army way. We're in 25th Company and live in Stable Row. The barracks are old brick stables and house over 200 gals apiece in double deckers. Our Platoon of 25 has a swell sergeant. I'm first squad leader for drill and fatigue duty. That means only that I'm one who has to "fall out" first, and I get to boss and assign the others instead of cleaning johnnies or scrubbing floors.

I love drill and we're getting pretty good. Think our platoon is the best of 25th Company, and of course the 25th is the best of the battalion. We march in platoon and company formation to everything we do, including mess and classes, and try to look like soldiers marching on ice!

Just learned how to fix our footlockers for first inspection tomorrow. Izzie's going to be our fun gal. She can never get her hands washed. Just about the time she gets back from something and ready to turn on the faucet, there'll be a command "Fall Out" and she comes a-running, jumps into her glamour coat and out into formation. It's really a panic.

Yesterday we got our real uniforms, and what an experience! It took only about an hour to get a full wardrobe—a barracks bag full of stuff, including the best looking kid dress gloves, wool gloves, hankies, galoshes, shoes, slips, pants. I look nifty in my uniform.

Yesterday we took aptitude tests, and this morning we had classification interviews. We're told that we shouldn't make up our minds as to what we want to do eventually, for we're likely to be disappointed. Then we rushed to mess after some outside drill, and had to swallow our sauerkraut and spare ribs on the double and get to the infirmary for more shots.

We were late, so marched down double-quick time, which for your info is 180 steps a minute. It's a workout. Try it sometime! Then, down the line with our sleeves rolled up and in about 15 seconds we had a smallpox vacination. Then our other arm was grabbed for a typhoid shot. We're beginning to feel like pin cushions. And, what do I think of it all? Really, I wouldn't have missed it for the world. They say if you can stand the first week of basic, you'll love it; and we have, and we do!

Just heard that for the last three weeks of our basic, our Company is getting moved downtown to the Chamberlain Hotel. We'll be living a more classic life.

WAAC News No. 3.
Fort Des Moines, Sunday, January 31, 1943

Yesterday we went to a lecture in the new theater in company formation—200 gals to a company, and almost 1,800 in all. Lieutenant Pugh said, "Company 25, file out, and don't pass out!" She's our company commander and a real honey—all culture, but with a lot of informality and a good sense of humor. And our sergeant is just tops. We'd do almost anything for her, and she tells everyone else that our platoon is perfect.

Friday was battalion inspection. The regimental officers [men] do it. Everything has to be shining and in the right spot. We have to know all the officers' names just in case one asks us. Liz got a gig for "hair too long," and this right after she'd had a haircut. Hair's not supposed to touch our collar!

After a lecture, we got our dog tags—two little metal tags with our name, address, serial number, person to be notified in case of accident, and "religion" stamped on. We wear them on a chain around our neck. Now we're really in the Army. Then we got our stamps, and everything we own has to be stamped with our name and Army serial number, so when we wash socks and they hang with dozens of others, we'll know which are ours.

Just after mess we were to have a drill competition, so we went for an hour's practice. Then had two minutes to go in and change our uniforms and march up to show off to the big shots. We placed second, and Sergeant Rice is sick because she'd gotten there late (which counted off) and had forgotten to face our platoon toward the inspection officer when she presented us, which is really an insult. We could all feel for her. We love her southern drawl and want to take her with us when we move, but that won't be.

Our GI clothes all go into a barracks bag. We wore our new uniforms for the first time and had to carry those bags a long way to the 18 trucks. The bags are lead! One gal jumps in the truck and all the luggage is shoved up to her. She piles it all down the middle with bags on top. Then we get in, five on each side. It's a chummy group.

The Chamberlain Hotel is right in downtown Des Moines. They did give us a chance to ask for roommates, and we three are together again. We have a second-floor room with one single and a double decker, and a kitchenette, which is something we didn't expect. The cafeteria is just off the main lobby. Meals are even better than on the post. We have silverware, glasses for milk, and jam and peanut butter always on the table. We're just stuffed most of the time.

After unpacking, mess, and a meeting, we were off last night. Even though Izzie was scheduled for KP tomorrow (our first day off!) we got her to go to a movie and saw Paul Muni in *Commandos Strike at Dawn*. Army sequences really come alive. At points I was thrilled to tears! We get into movies for half price, and all the stores show special privileges to WAACs.

Here we're off after five and on Saturday afternoons and Sundays. We'll drill at the Des Moines Coliseum about five blocks away, and have classes in another building. We're having quite a time learning how to salute officers. It's hard to know when and how to do it on the street, and when to just stand at attention in restaurants and such. I'm surprised that I like this stiff organization part. In civilian life we couldn't have done in three weeks what we did last week.

WAAC News No. 4.
Chamberlain Hotel, Des Moines,
Tuesday, February 16, 1943

The last two weeks have been hectic. Had our first battalion inspection. Got through OK. Then we had regimental parade, in which four battalions and twelve companies competed, and Company 25 (that's us) won! We were so thrilled, for we were the only Company of basics and had had only one week of that kind of drill. We had to go back to the Coliseum and have a dozen pictures taken. They just may send one to your paper. If so, I'll be in the front row on the left.

Then we got our second typhoid shots and a typhus,

which stings like the dickens. We were told to keep flexing our left arms to get the circulation going and relieve the sting. That got me into a funny kind of technical violation. Liz and I were walking back to the Chamberlain, me on the left. All of the sudden there was an officer coming toward us. There was no time to think, and since I'd been exercising my left arm, I saluted from the left as Liz did from the right. Thankfully, it brought nothing more than a big grin on the captain's face!

Eleanor Roosevelt is to pay her first visit to Des Moines, together with Colonel Oveta Culp Hobby, the Commander in Chief of the WAAC. Saturday morning we had practice formations at the Coliseum. I was drilling our squadron. It was pretty crowded and I nearly ran them smack dab into a wall before I could get out an "About Face"!

Then we went outside—all two thousand of us—parading in company formations by platoons, to the cadence of the super WAAC band. We marched around the block, over the Des Moines River, around another few blocks and back. It was below zero, and we had to wear our rayon socks and dress gloves.

The Sunday parade for Eleanor went off in grand style. It was still cold. She spoke to us as we stood in formation. We were told later that some in the audience had pointed to one Company and said, "Hey, look! Aren't they neat!" It was us! There was a big, really impressive picture of us in the paper.

I haven't told you about our classes. We have about six hours a day, one hour of physical training, one of drill. We had Military Courtesy and Custom, Current History (they know we don't have time to read newspapers, so they read them and tell us what's going on outside), Supply, Army Organization, and Articles of War. In many they have talkies, usually with movie stars as characters.

We've just started some new courses—Military Sanitation and Hygiene, Map Reading (which I love), and Defense against Chemical Attack, so we'll know about gases and how to wear gas masks and will go through a gas chamber; and also Defense against Air Attack, where we learn how to recognize all the different planes in the air.

Have been on KP twice and it's really something. You're on all day from 5:45 A.M. to 6:30 or 7:00 and have one hour off morning and afternoon. The first time I was in the kitchen and peeled onions, fixed baked potatoes, snapped beans, swept a cellar, mopped the cafeteria, shoveled coal, and washed pots and pans. Some pots are like wash boilers and up in size.

The second time I was in the dining room, setting tables, sweeping, mopping, and controlling traffic. We all live in fear of being on GI cans, where you empty and scrub the huge cans, strain the garbage and such. You should hear those who've done it tell the story. I've been appointed fire warden for the whole second floor and have to see that all rooms are cleared, cigarettes out, lights out, etc.

Basic is soon coming to a close. We hear LRs [latrine rumors, and the latrine is the john] that we may get assigned at the end of this week. We're all sweating it out! Had individual interviews last week. Those of us who wanted to apply for Officer Candidate School were interviewed by four officers asking such questions as, "If you had a gal who consistently came in drunk, what would you do? If you were on a troop train with a gang of gals, and at one of the stops one missed the train, what would you do?' It was quite an experience. Our company officers asked all three of us to apply, and we did. Now we'll have to wait.

As to assignments, we're told you can usually get into what you want later, but first you take what you get and do a good job. There's one big joker. Everyone lives in fear of being assigned to Cooks and Bakers!

2 Radio School

Because of the demands of the move, I did not write again for a couple of weeks about that difficult period of "sweating out" my future in the WAAC.

WAAC News No. 5.
Kansas City, Missouri, March 9, 1943

Well, here I am sitting in Room 214, Aladdin Hotel. I'm here for thirteen weeks to learn the Morse Code dit das if I don't get washed out of Army Radio School, and I don't intend to.

That week of waiting was a nightmare. On Wednesday Liz went off to Administrative School at Conway, Arkansas. On Friday Izzie got her orders for Administrative School at Nacogdoches, Texas. I'd applied for Administrative School too, since that's the kind of experience I'd had. But as they and others departed in various directions, I still wasn't one of them! Imagine how I felt when, on Saturday, those of us who had been kept at the Chamberlain were sent back to the fort. To add insult to injury, we were immediately put on KP. But that night I finally got my orders for Radio School at Kansas City. At first I was disappointed, for I'd pictured myself in Administration; but soon, as others were envious because they had wanted radio, I realized what a great opportunity it was. It was nice to think that I must have shown some special aptitude.

We left Des Moines at nine Saturday morning, and when we pulled next to the Rocket, it was fun to see all the people crowded at the windows to watch the WAACs detrain. In the depot we got the same onceover.

Company officers and several sergeants welcomed us

and marched us the mile and a half down the streets to the Aladdin. We're right in the Hotel District—a block from the new 4 million dollar city auditorium in which we drill.

Can't believe it, but we have regular hotel service! Rooms are cleaned, beds made, army style. We get clean towels, soap, hotel stationery, matches, and have a telephone in the room. Room keys are turned in each evening. All we have to do is keep our clothes hung up, shoes out of sight and stuff neat, except when we have formal inspection. Then drawers are open, we make our beds, etc. But that's only once in two weeks. The C.O. comes in and turns on our light in the morning when we're supposed to get up. We "fall out" into formation in the hall, and then have ten minutes to leave the hotel to go to breakfast, but not in formation!

The Keystone Building, where classes are held, is just a block from the mess hall. We have to get to classes by eight in the morning. At night we have room check at 10:45 and bed check at 11:00 P.M. except for Saturdays, when it's 2:00 A.M. And they mean business! Two minutes late for bed check or late for anything at all, and you're AWOL and can be up for dismissal.

Up to this morning we were allowed to wear civvies, and I was just bemoaning the fact that I'd sent mine home, when Lieutenant Tucker told us this morning that something had happened with a WAAC in civvies, and until further notice none would be worn! So that's that. No passes or furloughs till we've been here nine weeks, and then not for further than 360 miles. Pretty stringent, but there's lots to do around here.

Now for school. We're not in classes with the fellows, but they use the same rooms. We're students in the Midland Radio School—the leading one in the country that trains all Army radio personnel, and even personnel for commercial airlines.

And listen to this! The Army is allowed three dollars a day for our maintenance, and because they've been able to

The rror

---

make such good arrangements, they can save fifty-five cents a day on each of us. So they're giving that to us—sixteen dollars a month extra! Then, when we can send fifty-one words a minute, we get our corporal's (or T-5 for fifth-grade technician) stripes and sixteen dollars *more* a month. Forgot to mention that "51 words a minute" means Morse code, the dot/dash code one sends with a key like the guys at the train depot.

We go to school from eight to four, with an hour off for lunch.This first week we have had four hours of code. They're trying a new method on us, where we don't learn the dit-das (dots and dashes) but listen to them and associate the sound with a word. We have two hours of taking code in typing and an hour of printing by hand in a special way. I'm reminded of Gregg shorthand, for we have to learn special abbreviations, like AR = end of transmission, B = more to follow, F = do not answer, G = repeat back this entire message. When we're through at four, we're through for the day. That isn't hard to take! I thought we'd be studying our heads off.

I understand there are at least four servicemen to every WAAC around here, so one can have a date any time. Haven't explored that too much as yet, for I've gotten in touch with Ag, my Portland friend who married a Navy flier just before Christmas and moved to K.C. Right away Monday night I was invited there for dinner. Walt was out on a flight. I just got to talk with him over the phone. I'm to see a lot more of them.

I had a round-robin letter from OPA in Portland with notes from twenty-one of the girls and guys. Remember their job is to control prices. Virginia said,

Butter, meat, and fuel oil are all guaranteed headaches. You'd have laughed had you heard Mrs. L "releasing a pound of butter" the other day for an old man. . . . Everything has gotten so cut and dried—by the numbers now—so different than the kind of big happy family feeling we had when you were here.

WAAC News No. 6.
Aladdin Hotel, Kansas City, April 6, 1943

For my stay here I'm acting staff sergeant and have to
wear my stripes. That takes a lot of sewing, and it's hard
to get them on straight. You wonder what staff sergeant
means? Well, each section (ours has fifty gals) needs
someone to keep them posted on anything and everything, be responsible for all they do, see that they get to
classes, conform to regulations, etc. There are five buck
sergeants under me. Each of them is responsible to me
and the tech sergeant for their squad, and we are responsible to the company officers. In the morning at reveille I
call for reports from each of the sergeants. They salute me
and give their reports. Then I return their salute.

We have to drill the whole group once a week at the auditorium, and we always have a lot of spectators around.
It's really fun wearing the stripes. Never a day passes but
what the fellows yell, "Hi sarge!" Once in a while the guys
will salute me just to be funny.

Heard that the first class of WAACs that graduated here
three weeks ago have been sent to the Air Corps for duty.
We're hoping we will too. You'll notice I've not mentioned
officer training. We've heard nothing, and we've learned
that no one applies for OCS from here any more; that
would mean that all this training would be for naught,
and everyone seems to like the radio bit.

I'm working on twelve words a minute now and hope to
pass that soon. This week we started net procedure, where
we have to know how to open a network of stations, all the
special Army-Navy regulations, and use all those abbreviations and signals in calling other stations. We really know
what we've done when we finish seven hours of that; for
six of those seven we sit with earphones listening to dit-das.

WAAC News No. 7.
Kansas City, June 6, 1943

I'm too excited to settle down tonight, on account of we
got our orders. But we can't tell you when or where! I'm

lucky. Patty and I are going to the same place with two other operators and two mechanics. Patty's a good kid. We don't leave as soon as we had expected, so we have weekend passes. Portland sent us a cute little miniature version of *The Oregonian*. The June 3 headlines were "Yanks Chew Hole in Rome Barrier. 3,650,000 Soldiers Now Overseas." The article said, "Ground troops on overseas duty to hit 5,000,000." We hope to get overseas.

Last week was the most hectic I've ever gone through. About two weeks ago I passed the required test and made corporal (Technician Fifth Grade or T-5), so after I leave here I'll be Corporal Kochendoerfer to you. Though it may seem like a demotion (from acting staff sergeant), it meant a lot to me because I earned this one. Now I have to change the stripes on uniforms again. That ain't fun.

Then we were out on the nets. We'd go for special instruction from Sgt. Geoffrey from 10 to 12. Imagine sleeping till 9 bells in the Army! There we learn Q Signals:

QCA = You are causing delay by answering too slowly.
QCB = You're causing delay byanswering out of order.
QCD = What is the cause of delay?
QHF = Your frequency is slightly high.
QNW = May I close down?
QPZ = Affirmative "yes."
QQZ = Negative "no."

There are thirty nine whole pages of these!

Then we took our shifts on the nets, operating a radio station in one of the hotels from 1:15 to 7:15 without a break. There's a net of fixed stations in about 12 different hotels, which I was on Monday, Wednesday, and Friday. We had to learn how to tune and connect the transmitters and receivers and then keep the whole traffic rolling.

It was really fun when you got all the stations to come in, but a real headache to do it with a bunch of green operators. We had signals for frequency checks and almost anything one can think of, and it's *verboten* to send plain language over these wave bands. So it was thrilling when you'd send a message to the whole net and get a receipt for it. Made me realize how much they've taught us in just 12 weeks.

On alternate days we were on field stations set up in regular Army tents around this part of town. That was really something! They had three gals on—receiving and sending and a generator operator. Equipment all folds up, so as to be easy to move around. The generator is the funniest looking thing. It's a little tripod with a seat like a hobby horse. You straddle the thing and turn a kind of double crank, and have to keep it up all the time transmission is going on. Sometimes, with long messages, you're about ready to give up the ghost. And the field phones are so heavy and tight I was sure I'd come out a pinhead. Though it is against regulations, we always had lots of visitors. The fellows love to come and help turn the generator, which we don't mind at all. When we sent out for Cokes, they came back Coke highballs. Did they taste good!

On our last day when we came on duty at 1:15 P.M., we relieved fellows who had been on from 6:15 A.M., and we were supposed to be relieved at 7:15 P.M. It's a court-martial offense to leave your station before you're relieved. Come 7:15, Marge and I serviced our logs and then sat for fifteen minutes, getting angrier as the minutes passed.

I had turned my speaker on and some plain-language code came over, "Report in to Sgt. Geoffrey. No relief for station." and pretty soon, "Stay on duty till relieved." After stewing and trying to keep our own stations quiet and satisfied, we finally relaxed and started to enjoy it. Relief came at 8:30. The school had changed the schedule and not reported it to Army headquarters so they could arrange for our relief.

I missed a date and, after getting some late chow, didn't get back to the hotel till after ten. As I was starting to pack, the lights went out. Someone had blown a fuse on our floor. We all got together out in the hall and raised roughhouse, drinking Cokes and singing.

We Once were civilians, but now we are WAACs,
Dressed in our khakis, discarding our slacks;
Messing, saluting, with packs on our backs,
And our loves they are far, far away.

Oh, we'll become soldiers if it takes us years.
We'll stiffen our spines and we'll pin back our ears.
We'll tighten abdomens and tuck in our rears,
If that's what it takes to be WAACs.

When the lights finally came on, they said we could keep them on till late. That's how you happen to be getting this. And since it's perhaps the last from K.C., I must say we've surely had a swell time here. We've worked hard days and played hard nights. Take that as you will! Imagine I'll spend the weekend with Walt and Ag and will surely miss them! Just as one settles in and gets to feel at home! Such is Army life!

3 Assignment to Duty and Farewell

        Our "secret" destination turned out to be Char-
lotte, North Carolina. The day we left we celebrated with
lunch (and two daiquiris) at the Muelbach, a classy Kansas
City hotel I hadn't tried before. We boarded our train in the
late afternoon, and to our surprise we had a first-class draw-
ing room all the way through seven states—and then army
trucks for the last five miles to the base!

> **WAAC News No. 8.**
> **Sunday afternoon, June 13,**
> **Morris Field, Charlotte, North Carolina**

Here I am way down South! Been here since Thursday
morning and it's funny, but I almost feel at home already.
We arrived to find fifteen WAACs here, though there are to
be 150 eventually. We have two barracks, a mess hall, an office and recreation building with a great day room, where a
beauty parlor is just being installed. Our buildings have a
nice landscaped lawn, and behind us are rolling pine-
covered hills.

    After mess, Patty and I headed toward the radio aerials
and found the station with two great guys on duty; it didn't
take long before there were a dozen guys. The station here
is on the big War Department worldwide net on the AACS
[Army Airways Communications System]. To us it was exciting and almost bewildering with about five different stations coming in at once—some at 50 words a minute, some
at 15, all in different tones. It was actually scary!

    We later had our interviews with the communications
captain. Seems that now they have to await approval for us
from their headquarters in Atlanta. As a consequence, each
morning we report to a little civilian house near our bar-

racks, where they have receivers and stuff set up for practice work. We spend most of the time talking—doing very
little work. This net sends stuff really fast, and we're going
to have to speed up plenty in order to do the work if we're
approved. But when I remind the others, I get something
like, "Take it easy, Kochendoerfer, this is the Army!"

We're confined to the base for the first week, so I haven't
seen Charlotte as yet. It's a city of 100,000 and dry! So we
go to movies on the base, or the NCO [noncommissioned
officers] Club, where there's dancing. The club has been
ruled out to anyone under a corporal's rating, which leaves
out most of the other WAACs. Pretty undemocratic I'd say!
We get rides wherever we go in jeeps or scooters or tugs.
The guys always pick us up.

Bed check is at 2:00 A.M. on Saturdays and Sundays, midnight during the week, and there's always company. Practically every chap we've met so far has been a perfect
gentleman. It's unbelievable, especially after Kansas City.

Some of the guys at the station said they were being sent
overseas. Two said they don't want to go. "Five months
we've been here, and now that we're leaving they send you
gals in!"

Hope we get our assignments soon, or else get a furlough, for we have lots of time on our hands. Yesterday afternoon, after doing some code practice, Marty and I
decided to go to the PX. She's another shorty, with dark
hair, and just the kind of all-around person one would expect a North Dakotan to be. On the way we stopped to
watch the weather station send up a balloon. They're big
gray balls about two feet in diameter. As they let them go
they plot their course through a theodolite—a kind of sur-
veying glass on a tripod—calling readings down to the map
room, for the forecasting.

Marty and I said we'd like to see it through the theodolite. Since she's so short they had to lower it for her, then
raise it for me. In the process, they lost track of the balloon!
At this point the resourceful sergeant just made up readings to report to the map room. Later, when we went

down to check, the GI in charge said, "Hey, Sarge, what do
I do when the balloon goes off the map?"

I'm back from furlough nearly two weeks now. Marty, the
operator who lives in North Dakota, came back a day early
to spend the last day with me in Winona. We left from the
little station across the Mississippi over in Wisconsin. While
waiting we got the station agent there to explain the
switches and telegraph procedures, since we now felt part
of the show and could speak his language.

Back at Morris Field we had lots to catch up on—gossip,
new regulations, and such. Seems our authorization to operate on an Army Airways Communications Net still hasn't
been approved. They're afraid that since we're just WAACs
who enrolled, instead of being part of the regular Army
where we have to enlist for the duration, there may be
some kind of legal technicality. Now they think of that! In
the meantime, they've decided to start us in a course to
learn how to be link trainer instructors. We're to keep up
our radio just in case, but in the meantime we'll get this
other training, something we'd not counted on at all.

I'm sure you wonder what link training is. Well, it trains
pilots to make instrument landings in case of bad weather
or whatever. The trainers are like small planes fixed to the
floor, but turn and bank like a regular plane, have a full instrument panel and all the gadgets. When the pilot gets in
and puts down the hood, we talk to him by radio, wearing
earphones and telling him what to do, as we sit behind a
big desk with lots of controls.

If you were to listen in, you might hear: "Hello—Nan
Uncle, this is Able Baker Charlie—over," to which you
could hear us reply, "Hello Able Baker Charlie, this is Nan
Uncle." All this weird conversation just means that the
plane with the call letters ABC is calling Chanute Field, and
the field has answered.

Then the exercises cover all the difficulties and emergencies, like the weather, that make up instrument flying. We have dials at our instructor's desk that can make weather happen—like turning on a forty-mile-an-hour wind from the northwest, turning on rough air, or icing up the wings.

The lessons start out with straight flight, climbing and gliding with curves, spins, and stuff like that. One of the by-words around here is "get on the beam." This is where it comes from. The radio beam is like a huge cross on paper. The two sides enclosing the radio signal come together where they cross but keep fanning out getting ever wider the further out one goes. As a pilot flies toward a beam he hears the radio signal for an "n" (da dit). This gets louder and louder as he flies toward the beam. As he flies through the beam he gets a steady signal and, as he leaves, the opposite signal, or "a" (did da). Then as he leaves the beam he makes a 180-degree turn to come back through the beam, and continues this back and forth until the turns flatten out closer and closer to the beam and he finally comes to the "cone of silence," which is the airport, where the beams cross.

On our desks we have a big connected triangular recorder which has little wheels and accurately records the flight of the trainer. So when we're instructing we can have a big map of an area around an airport, and put the recorder down at any point, and the pilot has to orient himself by the beam procedure to finally bring his plane to the airport.

We just started a lecture course today. One of the sergeants put me in the trainer. After about ten minutes of regular flying, learning to use the rudders, ailerons, throttles, and elevators, making curves by remembering that one needle's width is three degrees, he turned on rough air, which comes in the eleventh lesson and just bounces you around while you try frantically to keep a straight course. It was scary, but I didn't do too badly. Of course he loved it! Oh yes, we're to get basics of Meteorology too.

I've been to Charlotte many times now, and go swimming a lot in this hot, muggy weather. No matter what we want to do there's always someone to taxi us around and share the fun. I've found a golfer from New York who has "ins" around here. He's tall, blond, and handsome, and knows it! As he drives for the general, he has special privileges and gets to fly all over and meet big shots. He loves to brag, but I can handle that.

WAAC News No. 10.
Morris Field Orderly Room, on duty as C.Q.
[Charge of Quarters, not dated]

A wire came the other day saying that we radio operators would be reassigned. They interpreted this to mean that we'll be transferred out of the Third Air Force, where we never should have been in the first place. But, as they say, "This is the Army!" So I don't know what's what just now. Will just have to wait and see.

Oh, I meant to tell you about last Wednesday evening when a B-17 a "Flying Fortress," landed on the field. We went out and got the crew chief to show us through before the guards got there. What a thrill! There are guns, and of course bombs, and oxygen tanks all through. It was fun to sit up in the cockpit now that we know what most of the instruments are all about. When you get into one of these big ones, you really respect the pilots. They have to know plenty.

❧

In that same letter there was a whole page about what Marty and I did socially. We had gone to one funny party at a private home where they had a hypnotist, and they really did have a guy rigid as a board lying with feet on one chair, shoulders on another and he didn't sag a bit. There were farewell parties for guys who were shipping out, evenings under the Carolina moon, and such.

But soon there was more to think about. In September 1943 the WAAC was to become the WAC, the Women's Army Corps. WAAC were given the choice of enlistment "for the duration" or discharge. We received this information in July and were to make an immediate decision. It was not an easy choice.

WAAC News No. 11.
Morris Field, 10:30 P.M., July 28, 1943

Hold your hat! I'm starting this letter, but don't know whether I'll ever send it or not. If I do, you'll have a big surprise. If I don't, you'll never know! But before I beat around the bush any more, I'll tell you and then go on to explain. I think I'm getting out of the WAAC while the getting is good! I know I've often bragged about being here, and never even hinted I had doubts, but I've thought of it ever since getting back from furlough. Marty's out already, and other gals have gone too.

It all came about when we had to sign up to make ourselves legal—that is, to enlist in the WAC, the Women's Army Corps. They gave us overnight to make up our minds. Just that afternoon Lieutenant Shaw had asked me to be guidon bearer—carry our company flag—in the parade when the new oaths are taken. Guidon bearer is an honor given to the gal who looks best in drill! But when we had to make up our minds so soon, I stopped and stewed.

A couple of the guys came over to see Marty and me. They had heard that all the squadrons were to be moved out and Morris was to become a WAC training center. That sounded grim; and if true, it's the last place I'd want to be.

Finally I decided not to enlist. The next morning I told Lieutenant Shaw she'd better find another guidon bearer, as I wouldn't be with the gals when they took the oath. Her reply: "Kochendoerfer, what's wrong? Why you're the last person I want to lose from this company!"

I told her my pet gripes—how I'd been in the Army seven months and hadn't done any significant work yet, how they kept shifting us from one thing to another, how we spent most of our energy on detail work around the barracks, running to the hospital for physicals, taking half a day off just to get ready for retreat parade. It almost seemed the Army didn't need us, that in fact we were a kind of diversion for the men. Worst of all, they'd just thrown an ultimatum at us to decide overnight. That's how I felt right then!

She was upset and did admit it wasn't quite fair. "I'll hold your slip and see Colonel Gates and tell him that he can't have us go through with it on the spur of the moment. I'll also call Captain Hill and tell him the same." Colonel Gates is base commander and Hill is in charge of operations.

Well! Captain Hill came into link that morning and asked for Corporal Kochendoerfer. We went outside and talked for half an hour. Captain or no captain, I told him just what I thought. He wanted to know whether I was dissatisfied with my work, and whether he could do anything to make me happier. I told him I was still waiting for real work. When I said I felt they should reorganize the Army, he admitted that they did lots of crazy things and wasted lots of good ability and money. He's a smoothy, though, and went on and on saying the WAACs are doing a great job and he'd take as many as he could get, etc. I knew I could discount most of his fast talk.

Well, that night at mess, Lieutenant Shaw announced that she had word from Colonel Gates that any girls who were undecided could wait until September 1 to make up their minds. She also cautioned us not to wear ourselves out worrying too much about barracks details. It really amused me no end. She had even called in one of the other girls I work with to find out whether she knew why I was feeling as I did.

The next weeks were plain hell, trying to make up my mind for sure. One day I'd decide to get out, as we'd spend a whole afternoon just sitting around and not doing a thing. Next morning I'd go up to the Line and see the flag flying and hear the bugle call and watch the planes coming in, and I'd think, "How can I leave all this and the swell friends I've made?" But then I'd remember that many of the best were leaving or getting out. Today I got to thinking that anything to which I gave my whole heart and soul had to be something I could believe in, and those I worked for had to be people I could respect. Those were fundamental things that came before flags and friends and stuff.

Many little things added up to my decision to get out. First and last, it isn't something I couldn't do. There's nothing hard about it all. Perhaps that's the whole thing, plus so many irksome details and regulations that might be necessary for guys going overseas—the discipline part, I mean—but it's all just a waste of time and energy for us gals, who could do a better job without the rules and regulations and discipline. I'm glad, though, for having given it a try, for I can now truly understand what Army life is all about, and even talk the language!

❧

That completed the volume of WAAC News. I'd written my favorite YWCA secretary, who was then in Baltimore, and Bob, a Portland boyfriend who was in the army in Liberal, Kansas. I'd asked their advice and especially appreciated things Bob said, writing on August 8.

I know exactly how you feel, because you're suffering from that very common human trait of spreading an aura of sentimentality over surroundings or persons we have been closely associated with. It's a common thing; but it does sometimes trick us into believing things that aren't true at all. Don't let it happen to you, Vi. Don't feel badly about not being able to make up your mind, either. You are the victim of mass psychology in the Army that is avoidable only by the most extreme sort of individualism.

You're not made to be one of the herd. If you'd decided to go to Officers' School I'd have been all for it, because (and I pay you the rarest of my compliments) you have that stature of mind and vision to see that your "men" come first, and should be given every priority and consideration. To me that's the first and most important element of being an officer. And too damn few have it.

On a lighter side, I did have quite an experience in link during those last weeks. Sergeant Duncan came up to me one day and said, "Kochendoerfer, do you want to take this pilot?" Since I hadn't actually taught any of the real pilots, I gasped but said, "Well, I might as well start sometime!" The pilot said he was on Lesson 5 and climbed into the trainer. I put on my earphones and megaphone. "O.K., all set?" "Yes, Ma'am." The guys felt the "ma'am" was a bit silly, but they had to use it.

The lesson was learning what to do if instruments failed. I had the student pilot counting cadence to use time at three degrees per second in changing headings. He started, "A thousand one, thousand two, thousand three," and kept this up until he had it right on the button to the second. Then I said, "Okay, you're flying due north." "Got it." "Now take a heading of 270 degrees and tell me how you'll do it." "I'll turn left ninety degrees, or thirty seconds," "Okay, start counting."

While all this was going on, a chicken colonel had dropped by, picked up a set of earphones, and plugged into one of the four slots in the desk where others could listen in. I thought perhaps he had flown in at the base and had time to kill. When at one point the pilot was having trouble, the colonel grabbed the mike from me and said, "hey, fellow, want to know an easy way to figure this out?" I didn't like his suggestion, so I grabbed back the mike. When this happened the second time, I said, rather pertly, "I'm sorry, sir. I've been told how to do this, and we're going to do it *my* way!" So we did.

After it was all over, Sergeant Duncan came up to me and said, "Know who that was, Vi?" Of course I didn't. "That was Colonel Eickelfritz, head of the 78th Group, in on an inspection tour." I took a deep breath and covered with a grin, but I felt pretty good later when I learned that the colonel had gotten a big kick out of being told off by a WAAC corporal and was telling everyone about it.

That's kind of an upbeat way to close my WAAC career. Now there was a whole wide-open life ahead and I decided to start the practice of seeing friends along the way each time I made a trip. So there were stops in Washington, D.C., Baltimore, Jersey City, and Greenwich Village in New York City before I headed home via Chicago. (In New York we stopped to read the big letters moving around the Times Square building: ITALY SURRENDERS.) After sharing my good adventures and the disillusionments of the past months along the way, I went back to hometown Winona, Minnesota, to wonder and wait for what was to happen next!

4 My Second Uniform

Never say never! I'd said it before, but this time I remembered, because I violated my own philosophy! After I'd been home a couple of weeks and seen all of my Winona friends, I took a job at the J.R. Watkins Company near our house—something I'd always said I'd never do! That was for those who stayed put after high school in comfortable office jobs. But I needed some income, so I used a good office typewriter to fill out an application to the American Red Cross.

The application asked for a degree in music or drama or such, and didn't even mention my kind of office and personnel experience. Yet the vision of possible overseas duty was enticing, and I must have felt I had a chance or I wouldn't have sent the letter. And glory be! I'd not been at Watkins more than three weeks when an air mail letter arrived saying I'd been accepted and would hear shortly about when to report to Washington.

The Red Cross would of course supply regular uniforms but sent a long list of stuff I'd have to provide, which they estimated would cost about $200:

6 blouses [style and color specified]
4 pairs plain black shoes [smooth leather oxfords, heels 1 inch or less]
4 pairs wrist-length gloves [style, color, and fabric specified]
1 black leather shoulder bag [inner pocket, no initials]
24 pairs stockings [neutral beige shades of nylon, silk, rayon, or wool]
2 sweaters [gray, white, or light blue wool, slipover, round neck]
1 bathrobe [dark all wool or part wool flannel]
1 pair bedroom slippers

6 bath towels and 2 washcloths
1 pair shower slippers and cap
6 sets underwear of choice [6 pairs panties (snuggies), at least 2
   wool or part wool and 4 cotton], 3 vests, 4 cotton brassiers, 6
   slips
12 handkerchiefs [white only]
6 pairs pajamas [2 warm, 4 cotton; one must be dark]
4 girdles [estimated year's requirement]
1 pair slacks [dark, preferably gray]
1 pair galoshes or short rubber boots
1 waterproof toilet bag with soap box, soap, cold cream, comb
   and brush, lipstick, deodorants, toothbrushes, toothpaste or
   powder, cleansing tissues.
6 doz. sanitary napkins, commpressed type; tampons, also space-
   saver; 6 yards best grade cheesecloth for emergency use
1 sanitary belt with safety pins
1 or 2 packs toilet paper [flat]
2 boxes shoe polish in kit, white and black.
1 extra pair eyeglasses if worn, and prescription
1 pair sunglasses [Polaroid or equal quality]
2 scarves [one dark for head with slacks on shipboard, one white
   for dress wear with winter uniform]
Name tapes [large] or indelible ink for marking clothes
1 flashlight with extra batteries and bulbs
1 footlocker, Army [31½ X 18¼ X 13¼], from RC uniform depot
1 suitcase [not to exceed 7 pounds empty or 40 when packed]

Suggested Supplementary Equipment: Bathing suit; leather for
resoling shoes with heels and nails; metal mirror; 3 T-shirts; fountain pen and pencil with eraser; ink in unbreakable container or
tablets or powder; Boy Scout knife; ball of cord; small hammer; bottle opener; can opener; nails; clothes bag and hangers; paper cups
or collapsible metal cup; sewing kit with scissors; notions: buttons,
shoelaces, pins and safety pins, bobby pins, hairnets, hairpins,
haircurlers; stationery; hot water bottle; short length rope or heavy
cord for clothesline; clothes pins.

For those social occasions when you want to get out of a suit but
must still be in uniform, a blue rayon jersey uniform dress has been
designed and is available for purchase at the Red Cross Uniform
Depot. Plain black pumps with medium heel may be worn with this
dress. No open toes.

Included in the many farewell parties was one at The Oaks, Winona's biggest night club. Our group of four arrived without reservations but was invited to join another farewell party at a large round table. Extra chairs were brought in, and I was seated next to George, the GI whose return to duty they were celebrating. He told me he was a gunner on the *Queen Mary*, which was being used as a troop ship. "I'll make you a bet," he said, "you'll be shipping out on the *Mary*." And just before leaving, he leaned over and said, "A deck, number seven." That was how I could find him if indeed we shipped on the *Queen*.

While waiting to go I had a letter from Bob, who was still stationed at Liberal, Kansas. He talked about the war and then went on to say that he wouldn't worry about my making a hurried or unwise choice of a man—however much I might eventually want a home and family—but counseled in closing: "I imagine (Hell! I know!) that you found yourself having to resist impulses to grant more than mere understanding to the fellows you met and liked at Morris Field. Right? You could see the situation through their eyes, because you yourself were disillusioned, and could really sympathize with them. But remember, that's a major factor in the moral let-down that comes with war; and I question seriously if the 'lines' the fellows use have much to do with it. Just a friendly warning."

I left Winona on February 28, 1944. In Washington I was to report to the Burlington Hotel. Rooms were $2.50 a night, for which we were reimbursed. We had time to poke around the capital between rather superficial training sessions at American University, having uniforms issued, and getting shots at the general dispensary in the Pentagon, Room 2D 201.

I was assigned to the club department overseas, which, at request of the military was to establish and operate on-base service clubs similar to the stateside USOs. After two weeks in Washington there was a week's extension training at a USO in Arlington Virginia, before we left for New York City. There we billeted at the St. John Hotel in Brooklyn. With some days to wait, we learned the subways so we could shop in Manhattan, try out restaurants, and see plays and operas—

Margaret Sullavan and Elliott Nugent in *The Voice of the Turtle,* *Oklahoma,* Paul Robeson in *Othello, Faust* and *Tannhauser* at the Metropolitan Opera (standing room only).

I couldn't understand the bundle of secrecy in which we were to wrap our identity and our leaving. We practiced for the big night several times, learning directions and what we would wear—which seemed to be everything we owned! On top of our winter uniform and red-wool-lined overcoat was our pistol belt, to which we attached canteens in little olive drab canvas covers, a gas mask, and other stuff, till we felt like Christmas trees! We were wearing helmets too.

The St. John was made up of several connected buildings. I was to go to the Pineapple Building at one signal, then at another to descend on a certain elevator and so on and so on. Finally we were picked up in army trucks and taken down to the dock—and there was the huge *Queen Mary* towering over everything; and supposedly everyone knew she was a troop ship! We boarded at night and set sail the next morning— Easter Sunday, April 9, 1944. Then we could see why the operation had to be so organized; there were thousands of troops, plus WACs and us. The members of our relatively small Red Cross group had an equivalency rank of captain, which meant we were to be treated like officers. So we drew the officers' sun deck, which was up top. When I heard that the WACs were somewhere down in the hold, I was surely glad I was now with ARC! I also heard that the GIs below had to sleep in shifts, since there wasn't room for all the guys to lie down at the same time.

At breakfast next morning we were reminded that the *Mary* was a British ship when we saw kippers on the breakfast menu: We couldn't complain about the food, though; for dinner on Tuesday, April 11, the printed menu offered Potage Rohan, Whitefish Poche, Sauce Riche, Braised Sweetbreads Florentine, Roast Vermont Turkey with Cranberry Sauce, French Beans, Fried Eggplant, Roast and Boiled Potatoes, and Plum Pudding with Sweet Sauce.

Louise Smith, whom I'd met at the USO in Arlington, and I became good friends of two Aussie officers who somehow were on their way to England. Rex was my type; we kept in touch, and I did see him again in London. And one afternoon Smitty and I had an invitation from British officers for tea in the *Queen Mary* ward room, but for me the festivity was cut short when my stomach rebelled.

After I regained my sea legs, I thought of George and "A deck, number 7." Even though we were restricted to our deck, I slipped down and after much inquiry found George "in the sack" following night duty. He was not allowed on the sun deck but said, "I'll meet you there at the dog kennels. If some officer spies me, I'll tell him you're my long-lost cousin!" So we'd meet there and have long conversations. George explained that we were in a convoy and that the *Mary* zigged and zagged and was blacked out at night. Together we dreamed up how I could cover my hair and join him one night on gun duty, but a steward appeared at the spot we'd planned to meet, and that plan didn't come off.

The crossing took ten days; we arrived April 19 at Greenock in Scotland. The *Mary* anchored a long way out in the harbor, and we had to go in on tenders. The one I was on was held up, sitting out in the harbor in a freezing drizzle, but finally we landed and immediately boarded a train for London. The train was blacked out, with every opening sealed tight, and what with hundreds of military jamming the coaches, whooping it up and smoking, I ended up losing my voice. This turned out to be a plus, as it ensured me a warm room with steam kettle in London while the others had their first taste of what "cold" could mean in England in their unheated dormitory rooms.

We were in London about a week. After I had my voice back, I went out on a date with an officer I'd met. No buzz bombs that night, but in the fog and the blackout one had to really feel for curbs and corners of buildings to avoid stumbles and collisions. Along the way, standing out in the blackness, I noticed tiny red neon signs reading "PRO" with an arrow beneath pointing right or left. After seeing the third one, I said to my date, "they surely have lots of public relations officers over here!" I couldn't see the smile I know now must have been there as he said. "That's not a bad way of putting it! But here are the facts . . . " Later I was to fight the army, refusing to let them use my Red Cross club as a prophylaxis station, where GIs picked up supplies and treatment.

It was hard to believe I was actually in Britian. Even in the April spring daylight, London's atmosphere and buildings seemed damp and dark, though lightened with feelings of history. Since the American Red Cross had its British headquarters there, I would come to feel more at home in London, even sweating out buzz bombs, in the months to come.

PART II

Initiation to the Real War

5   Welcome to England

As newcomers to Britain, our GIs received a little newspaper with a big photo of Churchill and his words under the huge letters WELCOME!

To each American soldier who has left home to join the great forces now gathering in this island, I send a message of greeting and welcome. Wherever you may go in our country, you will be among friends. Our fighting men look upon you as comrades and brothers in arms. Welcome to you while you are with us; and when the time comes we will all go forward together and carry the good cause to final victory.

The paper went on to say, "And now, here's big news since you left: Russians Regain Crimea; Fall of Sebastopol Near." Among other articles on the front page was "Finns Reply to Russia Soon," suggesting that their reply to Moscow's latest peace terms would be to reject them. On the back page the leads were "Jap Attacks in Burma"; "Italy Not So Quiet"; "Eleven Axis Ships sunk in Adriatic"; "Airmen Busy in Pacific"; "US Warns Finns to Break with Germany"; "Nazis Hold Sofia"; "Constanza Raid by Russians"; "Spain Grabs Oil."

A big map of the British Isles was captioned "Come right In—this is Britian. Glad to have you with us!" The text pointed out the smallness of the British Isles: "The U.S. is 26 times as big. Maximum distance North to South is 875 miles."

One article of great help was "How Much in Ours Is Yours?"

To find the value of one shilling in American currency, divide the rate of exchange of 20, thus: at 4.60 dollars to the pound, one shilling equals 23 cents. A one pound note is equal to 20 shillings. Write ten Shilling note (10/ or 10s). Coins: Penny (1d); halfpenny (½d) pronounced 'Haypenny'; farthing (½d); three penny bit (3d) pronounced 'thruppenny'; two coins, one silver, the other brass alloy; sixpence (6d); shilling (/ or 1s); florin, or two-shilling piece (2/ or 2s); half-crown (²/₆ or 2s6d). Bronze coins are usually called coppers. 'Three and six' means three shillings and sixpence.

It took some practice to get from holding out a handful of change so a cabbie could take his fare to being able to tell quickly whether a sign in a store window promised a real bargain, or to keep books and reconcile thousand-pound revolving funds in pounds, shillings, and pence. All that was to come later.

Our own War and Navy Departments also put out "A Short guide to Great Britain for Military Personnel Only." It began:

You are going to Great Britain as part of an Allied offensive—to meet Hitler and beat him on his own ground. For the time being you will be Britain's guest. The purpose of this guide is to start getting you acquainted with the British, their country, and their ways. America and Britain are allies. Hitler knows that they are both powerful countries, tough and resourceful. He knows that they, with the other United Nations, mean his crushing defeat in the end. So it is only common sense to understand that the first and major duty Hitler has given his propaganda chiefs is to separate Britain and America and spread distrust between them. If he can do that, his chance of winning might return.

The long guide was invaluable in many ways. After describing the British government, customs and manners (like driving on the left and preferring warm beer), love of sports, and indoor amusements in the pubs, plus providing an invaluable glossary of terms, it went on:

[Don't rub] a Britisher the wrong way by telling him "we came over and won the last one." . . . Britain remembers that nearly a million of her best manhood died in the last war. America lost 60,000 in action. The Briton is just as outspoken and independent as we are. But . . . he is also the most law-abiding citizen in the world, because the British system of justice is just about the best there is. There are fewer murders, robberies, and burglaries in the whole of

Great Britain in a year than in a single large American city. When you find differences between British and American ways of doing things, there's usually a good reason for them.

At home you were in a country at war. Since your ship left port, however, you have been in a war zone. Britain has been a war zone since September 1939, which has brought great changes in their way of life. Every light in England is blacked out every night and all night. Every highway signpost has come down. Barrage balloons have gone up. Grazing land is now ploughed for wheat, and flower beds turned into vegetable gardens. The peacetime army of a couple hundred thousand has been expanded to over two million. From the biggest factory to the smallest village workshop—all are turning out something for the war. Hundreds of thousands of women have gone to work in factories or joined the many military auxiliary forces. Old-time social distinctions are being forgotten as sons of factory workers rise to be officers in the forces and daughters of noblemen get jobs in munitions factories.

In the next ten months I was to value that good information and advice and would learn through experience that with all our differences, humans around the world have more things in common than differences. And then, I thought, perhaps learning this by sharing a war would bring a deeper understanding of it than people could ever achieve in peacetime or as tourists.

My real initiation to this new learning began when I was assigned to fulfill a request from the 315th Troop Carrier Group for a Red Cross service club on their base at Spanhoe Airdrome up in the Midlands between Peterborough and Leicester. I was ever to wish, however, that the ARC had been as thoughtful in providing background information and advice on how to open, staff, and run a base club. That lack was to become obvious after an earlier—and abortive—assignment.

In late April 1944, I was off alone to begin my new adventure. Orders said to be on a train leaving Liverpool Street Station that afternoon for Cambridge. I was to replace a Red Cross club director on a military base near there, and Art Coster was to be my field director.

My family had been notified of my safe arrival, but I was not allowed to tell them of my whereabouts in Great Britain. In my first short letter, however, I invented a Kochendoerfer code whereby combining the first letter of each word following a comma or period would tell them where I was. I described my short time in Cambridge (for the director there changed her mind and decided to stay) and told them that before leaving I'd had time to explore the campus of a famous university and had tea one day with the British manageress of the club. She pointed out that the elderly chap at the opposite table was none other than Bertrand Russell. "He often teas here," she said.

Upon arriving at my next home, I shared the experience in detail with family and friends, after I was made the great gift of a portable and supplies and could make carbon copies.

Somewhere in Great Britain, May 12, 1944

Art Coster picked me up at noon and we were off. The rolling countryside is so pleasant and homey, just like the pictures you see—little villages every couple of miles, with tiny thatched or tile-roofed cottages along winding narrow streets, with hedges on both sides of the road in the open country. Each village has a picturesque church and one or more pubs with the craziest names, like "The Bull and Hare" or "The Red Cow." And of course we came at the right season, as Browning said, "Oh, to be in England, now that April's here!"

Coster is a fine chap. One the way he tried to tell me a few things I was about to face. I was to open a new club all by myself. It was not to be an "aeroclub" like the one in Cambridge that offered a snackbar with sandwiches, but a "donut dugout" where we'd serve only donuts, coffee, and Coke. He said some supplies and equipment were there, and more would be coming in the days ahead. It all seemed so nebulous I couldn't even think of intelligent questions to ask.

We finally arrived at an airdrome, named after the big farm that used to be there. The base is expansive and impressive. After stopping at headquarters for my introduction to the commanding colonel (where I was told I would eat at the officers' mess and where it was), we drove to the plant that is to be my donut dugout.

I was floored! It was practically a little town of drab Quonset huts spreading in several directions. Coster said it had been built for a NAAFI club (meaning Navy, Army, Airforce something or other) when this was a British base, but it had never been used. The British NAAFI is like our Army's Special Services, which provides movies and social events and personal assistance for the men. Now the American Red Cross was to take over the running of clubs when one was requested by a military group.

The plant consists of one huge building at least half a block long. Inside there is a lovely stage with velvet curtains at one end, and a space at the back which can be used as a dressing room. There's a big serving area with a long counter on one side, where we'll dispense the donuts, coffee, and Cokes, and a huge light kitchen extending behind. Off the kitchen are three storage rooms, a lovely corner room that I'm taking for my office, another office for the manageress when I get one, lavatories, etc.

Two more large Quonsets are connected to this huge one by little passageways. One of these, as big as the whole aeroclub at Cambridge, I think will be our game room, for it does have a pool table. The other is divided into three smaller rooms and may be a lounge, library, writing room. But before you envision straight walls with a conventional roof, let me remind you that it's a big mess of Quonset huts—those rounded buildings of corrugated metal, with the windows sticking out along the side like little dormers. From a distance it looks like a bunch of farm buildings. My quarters are in a smaller Quonset just across a back court.

As we stood outside, Coster's parting words were "Here are the buildings, Vi. Open up a club. I'll be back in a couple of weeks to see how you're doing." As he started to drive away, he leaned out and added, "Oh, by the way, the first thing you'd better do is hire yourself a British staff!"

I'll not forget the "gone" feeling I had as he drove off. I just stood there. Questions buzzed in my mind. "Staff? How Many? Where will I find them?" I entered my starkly furnished room, sat down in the one chair, and once again began to wonder about it all. Finally, in unpacking, I realized it was time for chow. I had never felt quite so alone as I did walking down the dirt road and into the officers' mess for dinner. Heads turned one by one as they saw an American woman. It would be interesting to know some of their reactions. I'm sure I'll find out when I get to know them. Two officers took me to the movie after chow, and one walked me back to my quarters.

I opened the door as we said goodnight and flicked the switch. Nothing happened. Seems the electricity hadn't been turned on in that building. So we walked over to the nearby Post Exchange while the officer took one of the GIs back to investigate. They couldn't do anything, so we called utilities. It was Sunday. There was no answer.

At the PX the sergeant in charge and I had a little party with some coffee, toast, jam, and cookies. He said that if there's anything I want or need, all I have to do is ask. Then he gave me his flashlight to take back with me, by laying it on a nearby chair, I was able to unpack more of my stuff.

Next day I walked into that huge expanse of empty space in the big Quonset. I felt so small, shivering alone in the cold. Looking at the raw concrete floor, I truly wondered how this could possibly become the kind of club I had envisioned. Just what I'd expected I wasn't sure, but it wasn't this.

Then I recalled what Coster had said: "Hire yourself a British staff." But again, how many? for what? from where? I decided I'd better talk with someone on the base. I walked out to the road. A passing GI offered to take me to the supply officer, but "first you better stop by the motor pool to see about some kind of wheels." I was to get no vehicle of my own. When I wanted to go somewhere I was to call the motor pool, and some kind of vehicle and driver would be dispatched. With the supply officer I made arrangements to get paint for the walls and the concrete floors, but no one offered the manpower to do the work. On the way back I stopped some GIs who came along and asked whether they had time off and would be willing to come help. It worked! I had several to scrub and clean up the place before we got to the painting.

That second evening after coming back from chow, I stood in the doorway of one of the smaller Quonsets which was filled with furniture piled nearly to the ceiling. As I stood there in the silence, the oddest thing happened. I suddenly sensed another presence and turned to find a handsome, grinning master sergeant. "I heard about your budding operation and came by to check things out." He was no less than John Stetson III, sergeant major of the 315th Troop Carrier Group, one of the best guys to get to know. He could pull lots of strings.

As we talked, I mentioned that I was almost tongue-tied without a typewriter—and glory be, I live a charmed life! Imagine hearing, "Think I can take care of that." Next day he came over with a portable he said I could keep; you can thank him for getting this typed letter. As sergeant major, John also had the power to provide details of men when we got to the painting stage. Another plus—he put me in touch with Captain Conquest.

That touch was magic! Conquest cut through Army red tape and got things going. I'd asked for a bicycle and fatigues (the olive green coveralls the guys wear around the base), but nothing had happened. He told one of the sergeants to go get a pair of fatigues from the quartermaster, then turned to another officer and commanded him to do the same about a bike.

At mess this noon Conquest had a grand idea about the paint job. He said, "Go see Captain Horner. He has an air compressor and some spray guns." Horner said I could have it tomorrow afternoon, but when Conquest heard that, he said, "We'll go get it now." I got in the car, and we hauled the compressor over and got the job started. Conquest is a "can-do" guy!

Then we went back to pick up my bicycle. The guys think I look cute in my fatigues, even though they're far too big. And I have to learn how to ride these bikes. They have brakes on the handlebars. Remember the bikes we rode with coaster brakes, where we'd stop by stepping back on the pedal? Now if I do that, I just find myself pedaling backward and going ahead!

Conquest asked me to go pub-crawling with his bunch. They go on bicycles, and it must be something like we used to do on Saturday night back home, going from one place to another. Only the pubs here are farther apart, at little towns or out in the country.

❧

I learned that later ARC did get around to providing manuals to beginners like me, with a handbook of some kind on "how to open a donut dugout." I could have helped them write such a handbook, because I learned the hard way. There were ever more questions about supplies and rules and regulations, and so many hows and whats and whens that I truly wonder how I did it. I shared some of my frustrations along the way with family and friends, when I had time days later.

Somewhere in Great Britain, May 21, 1944

Got my phone today. Now we can call all over the country but instead of an operator making the connections, you get the nearest town and tell that operator who you want to talk with; she plugs you in the next leg and you tell them the same thing. This goes on, and sometimes the connections get broken and you have to start over. If this sounds time consuming and frustrating, that's just the way it is.

Tonight went over to the PX for some kindling and got my weekly rations—seven packs of cigarettes, two chocolate bars, two packs of gum, soap, fruit juice, cookies, matches. Women can get cosmetics and things, which are rationed too. In addition to regular weekly rations we'll get a few bobbie pins every so many weeks, one small box of Kleenex a month, etc. Tonight I came out with an extra Hershey, a bottle of Coke, a promise to go golfing at a swell club near here, and a guy named Joe to come over and build fires in the clubs. After that, and my experience with John Stetson, I have to be careful. If I say, "I surely wish I had . . ." someone pops up with it.

I'm learning how to get things from the Army. Being a civilian, I can barge in to see any officer without the usual formalities and don't have to mind my p's and q's too much. And looking for help has become both a huge head-ache and a lot of fun. For transportation I have to call the motor pool and can still see Jim reporting for duty the first time in his clean but wrinkled fatigues, and a round-brimmed cloth hat smashed down on his reddish blonde hair. His blue eyes were anything but smiling. He may have been kidded for having to drive "that Red Cross wom-an" around.

I asked Jim, "What's the nearest village?" "Uppingham is about eight kilometers over that way." "OK, let's go." This was a route we were often to traverse in his command car in the months to come. The road wound over the roll-ing countryside, at one place going down a long hill with a railroad track at the bottom, then turning upward again. The Brits have the practice of closing gates across the road long before the train comes, and not opening them for a time afterwards. GIs on bikes, feeling no pain on the way home from a pub crawl, would often come sailing down that hill oblivious of the gates and crash through. The Army paid for so many repair jobs that the bike became known as "Hitler's secret weapon."

We have the darnedest times following these English di-rections, which they're always so eager to give. "You bear around a bit to the right, take the next turn to the left, and you'll see a little lane . . ." Or, often, "then you'll come to a roundabout . . ." They invariably end with "You *can't* miss it!" That's a standing joke over here. But Jim and I *have*, ending up in cow pastures, estates, and other interesting spots.

In searching for a staff, I had the best luck stopping at the village post offices to inquire whether they knew of anyone wanting a job. That's how I learned that I'd be able to hire only women over a certain age; the rest were required to be in the military or defense work of some kind. In Uppingham, the postmaster thought a while and said, "Come to think of it, there's a Mrs. Dolby. You might ask her. Tell you how you'll get there." Then those directions again. Things looked up when we bagged Mrs. Dolby, but there were many dry runs and disappointments to come before we had our staff of fifteen Brits.

Every once in a while in driving around the beautiful countryside, I say to myself, "And I'm getting paid for this!" Another bonus was getting into British homes, talking with the people and just learning to know England. At one place on a cold day I was invited in for tea, which sounded plenty good. So I got Jim to come in too, but only after much persuasion. Ever since, though, he's with me all the way.

With my work schedule I don't have time to accept all the invitations. There's a convalescent home near here where I can go for tennis, horseback riding, and swimming if I ever have time. I have seen the countryside from the air, too—in one of our C-47s, the Army's workhorse with metal bucket seats along each side where troops or paratroopers sit in transport. From the air it's like a patchwork quilt, with tiny fields all embroidered together by hedges. I sat with my nose pressed against the window every minute. Next time I want to get up to the cockpit and watch them fly the plane.

As I said, days are full. You can't imagine the millions of details involved before a place can be opened. And in the Army, except for the Captain Conquests, everything takes about six contacts to get done. If I want leaks in the roof fixed, shelves put up, lights, locks, windows fixed, ashes hauled, coal, or things like that, I call our Utilities Sergeant. He makes out a form and takes it to the British chief (there's a British complement on base) who says "yes" (or "no"), gives it to the British clerk of the works, who gives it to a civilian, who does the job. Today I have three fixing up quarters for the manageress, who will live with me. They're painting the bathroom floor, leaving little paths to the john and basin. Tonight I'll paint myself out after I use them.

∿

It took some time, but I finally had a core staff to start with and had hired a manageress sight unseen upon good recommendations from her fellow Britons. On May 16, 1944, I had received word by telegram: "ARRIVING HARRINGWORTH STATION WEDNESDAY 11:15 AM. MASON."

Miss Mason was a tall, thin, washed-out blonde who looked the typical Briton I'd pictured over the years. She knew the ropes of her war-torn country and was a big help, since I had so much to learn. She also knew how to handle the staff; she could speak their language and commanded their respect.

To begin with, Miss Mason told me I'd have to go to a certain office in Stamford and buy two sets of stamps to paste in little books for each age group of employee. They were tuppence or thruppence or sixpence stamps, depending on the employee's age. One set was for old age pension, another for health insurance, I think it was. It was like filling S & H Green Stamps books; remember those?

By telephone from London I learned that I'd received a thousand-pound revolving fund—close to $5,000—from which to pay the help. But that wasn't the only money I'd have to contend with. Each day I had to take in cash at the club from the GIs, because General Eisenhower decided that since our men received better pay than the Brits, they needed to pay for their donuts and coffee and Coke. He felt they'd appreciate it more if it weren't free. I agreed with him there, even though it meant keeping track of this income and going to the bank in Uppingham regularly with deposits.

May 21, 1944 (continued)

Yesterday I had to make arrangements for feeding the British staff, who were to have one meal on the base. First we were told to get prepared food from the mess and bring it over here. Then the adjutant decided we could use a room at the mess hall. But this morning the mess officer called to say, "No, you'll have to get the rations and cook them at your club," whereupon the quartermaster said that was against regulations. Believe it or not, the last story was that they couldn't feed them at all if they didn't live on the base. At that point I called our Red Cross headquarters and found out it was the Army's responsibility. Finally, with that information, the commanding colonel promised they would feed the staff at the mess hall. So in the morning I have to go up and clear that with the mess officer. I'm glad I can do it as a civilian!

Don't get me wrong. Everyone is swell, but in these go-rounds you begin to wonder how we're ever going to win this war! Another problem. I haven't been able to find enough help in the villages close enough for them to bike in, so the adjutant got me to present the case to the executive officer. As a result, I think I have transportation promised so that I can go to a larger town and hire a bunch (I hope) and have Army transportation for them.

They've also promised to put a GI on permanent assignment to build fires and do odd jobs, and a detail each morning to clean the place, till I get enough British help. And I have run into sources of volunteer help. I've been invited to tea several times, and as one woman said, "If you can come all the way across the Atlantic to help, the least we can do is try to help you."

I've learned another "woman's way" of asking for things. At the officers' dance Monday night I'd say to my partner, "Now's the time I should ask you for . . ." He'd listen and say he might not remember, but I should call him next day. It worked! The custodial officer, who has charge of all unexpendable things, gives me everything I ask for and more. In addition to furniture for the manageress's room, I got to looking around and came out with two extra bookcases, a heavy scale, a hatchet, a soap dish for the bathtub, and several other things they weren't using that we needed. Yesterday when I went to the quartermasters for more rags to wash windows, the sergeant promised me another pair of fatigues—my size this time—and a flight jacket.

The engineers made me four custom doughnut cutters, and another fellow took my fatigues up to the line and washed them in gasoline to remove paint stains. He said he's going to write his family that "there's a woman over here who has me doing her laundry." This same chap was on detail earlier one day and wouldn't do a thing; now he comes around a lot, and I've got him working all the time. The guys kid me that every time they come into the place, I put them to work. But they seem to like it and come back for more. We call them our Red Cross commandos.

One word about the pubs. You should taste this beer. It's called "arf and arf" (half and half) or "bitters" and is something like dishwater. I like an Irish beer called Guiness when we can get it. It's thick and nearly black, with lots of body. Mostly, though, the guys drink whatever they can get, and we feel lucky when we have "spirits" (Scotch). At the colonel's birthday party at the officers' club Monday night we had mixed drinks, but they're warm—with no ice. I started with rum and Coke, then passed up the gin and orange squash and had a Scotch, but refused wine. Sometimes they mix rum with ginger which is terrible. No wonder lots get drunk or sick.

❧

I kept wishing the club could be open and operating. Colonel Mac, the base commander, said so too. He was quite an outspoken Scot, though pleasant enough, with a deeply wrinkled craggy face, a mustache, and a trim pointy beard. One night at chow he asked about the grand opening. "If it isn't soon," he said with a grin, "I'll take those huts back and make barracks out of them!" I might have told him that had he offered more help sooner, it could have been open by then, but I still had to train a green staff how to make and sell donuts.

We got donut mix in big bags. It had to be mixed with water to just the right consistency, and the dough rolled out and cut by hand. Then the fat had to be just hot enough to make the donuts light and fluffy. I'm sure if you've ever fried donuts, it wasn't on huge wood-burning ranges in heavy, oblong iron kettles that looked like oversized roasters.

Another worry. We were sent just enough fat for the amount of donut mix—provided everything went without a hitch. But if the consistency of the dough or the fire temps weren't just right, we'd end up with grease-soaked sinkers that got so hard and heavy as they cooled that I'd throw them out, feeling too guilty to charge for them. Then we'd end up with mix but no fat, and headquarters didn't like that! I found time to write a few paragraphs home again.

Spanhoe, England, June 21, 1944

Well, since my new manageress has been here, I've been well taken care of. I don't get up early enough to eat breakfast at the mess, so she fixes me toast and coffee and even brought some eggs with her. They're a definite luxury over here; and the GIs make trades with the Brits to get eggs and milk. It's illegal to drink the unpasteurized milk for fear of undulant fever, but they do it.

Miss Mason is a good worker. When I have time, we sit and talk and compare notes. It's interesting what Americans and British find odd about each other. For instance, we think it's funny when signs tell you to "halt" instead of "stop," not to "overtake" instead of "no passing," and such. But they think our calling others by their first names is horribly familiar. They feel the way we eat is crude, while I think the way they shove or mash things on their fork with a knife looks as though they'd never been brought up right. Their "teaspoons" are small demitasse size, and "dessert spoons" are about as big as our tablespoons.

And then there's US Army tradition, which has now included me! The staff car Jim drives being overhauled, was out of service for several days. When he picked me up today, there was a bashful grin on his face as I noticed VIOLET in black letters outlined in red across the front. He said, "The guys did it." Then I remembered getting a phone call from a chap who asked me how I spelled my name and hung up. Most of the jeeps and trucks on the base have been named by the fellows, and I suppose I should feel honored to have a staff car named for me. Makes me feel silly though.

The Club Opening, Buzz Bombs, and D-Day

The last few days before the club's big opening were hectic. When I went to the bank in Uppingham to open accounts, the president took care of me in his private office. I had to call all over England to try to get a Coca-Cola contract, and when it didn't come through, I had to make special arrangements to buy Cokes in Uppingham for the opening. I returned from town to find Field Director Coster in my office, calling officers and ARC gals from other clubs and inviting them to the opening on Saturday. I'd had to get notices around the base and check with Colonel Mac, who said, "If you're not taken care of by the fellows, come to me with you problems!" I said to myself, "Now he tells me!" New staff was arriving each day and we had to get them oriented to their jobs.

Then something happened I couldn't believe: in the midst of all this I was offered a transfer. The field director said I couldn't tell anyone, and it would mean deciding by the next Tuesday, packing and leaving Wednesday. I was furious! How did they feel I could run out on the 315th right after the club opened? It wasn't a hard decision. I couldn't pour all this out in my letters home, but I did share the opening.

Spanhoe Airdrome, Midlands, England, June 28, 1944
The day we opened was really something. One of the mess sergeants sent over three cooks to help those I'd hired, and they made donuts madly all day. I chased around trying to get all the last things done and jumped into the tub at six, with the opening set for seven. I did tell Miss Mason that she'd have to handle the kitchen and snack bar, but there were always decisions to be made about something we'd not talked about.

Everything was free that night, and we had a mob of GIs. The base orchestra played, and though I wasn't satisfied, all were so loud in their praise that I guess it was strictly OK. The Red Cross visitors said it was one of the largest and nicest clubs they'd seen, and our invited officers were impressed at what we'd done with those sterile Quonset huts.

I'll be ever grateful to Tommy, one of the Brits from the small complement on the base, who can play anything on the piano; you just have to call it out. Eleven o'clock found about fifty GIs around the piano singing their heads off. From the far end of that long, long room I heard:

> I've got sixpence, jolly jolly sixpence,
> I've got sixpence to last me all my life,
> I've got sixpence to spend, and sixpence to lend, and
>   sixpence to send home to my wife, poor wife . . .

You know I sing good harmony, so I started down to join them. By then they'd started another song and were swinging it till they noticed me. Singing stopped abruptly, and all turned toward me. I asked, "Why did you stop?" One grinned and said, "We really don't know you yet." What they were singing was another favorite, with the refrain "Roll me over in the clover, "Roll me over, let me die, and do it again!" It didn't take long for them to feel they knew me well enough to sing it and even let me join in with the harmony!

❧

Red Cross had asked us to bring ascorbic acid tablets for our Vitamin C because we wouldn't be getting citrus fruit. But in the office I had the gift of two GIs, three oranges worth their weight in gold, and three cans of grapefruit juice had come from the mess sergeant. One of the boys even brought me a peach all wrapped in cotton. It had cost him the equivalent of nearly three American dollars. Some fellows told me they'd paid four or five pounds for a quart of gin before realizing it wasn't dollar bills they were spending!

The GIs were soon flooding into the club, which offered a

lot of good wholesome activities that didn't take a degree in something to set up or take part in. Bingo was popular, and the guys loved "Truth and Consequences"; they could think up hilarious consequences and got the biggest kick out of skits where I was involved—like a GI having to propose to me or, heaven forbid, kiss me! When we got a public address system, we made good use of the mike, for we sang a lot. I was pleased at how much it helped the shy guys. Once they heard themselves over the speaker, they'd be back in line waiting to do it again. And they loved my harmonizing; with a group, I'd get the mike so my voice could compete with theirs. I was pleased so many guys enjoyed it.

And did they love the donuts! The lines were terrific. They said we made the best coffee they'd had anywhere. I was working in the office one evening when a chap that had moved off the base was back. We had a chat. As he left, he stuffed a little note in my hand. "Don't read this, Vi, till I'm gone," he said and dashed out. It read: "To Vi, in memory of one of the nicest clubs in England. Our sincerest thanks and appreciation to you for all of the things you did to make us boys feel at home. The games, the donuts and coffee, not to mention the hospitality. We all say we enjoyed your club more than any other. Thanks again for everything. All the gang & Bill." I wanted to cry. You sit and think of all the stuff you could have done for them and didn't.

Another note left in the suggestion box mentioned said that since there wasn't a thing to do in town on a pass, it was no exaggeration to say that our club was the next thing to home in the ETO—suggesting that their barracks surely didn't qualify. I realized then that with most of the guys on base living in tents set on wooden platforms, our club did offer a comfortable place to be, with walls, light, heat, and space, plus food and a place to play pool and table tennis, and spots to sit down and write home. Red Cross furnished stationery for the men. It was about the color and texture of brown paper bags—as was our toilet paper, which I once used for stationery, writing, "Thought I'd send you a sample of our Scottissue so you can see (as we say) 'It's rough in the ETO!'"

These *were* rough times for GIs, and since we didn't have a field director on the base, I was Red Cross to the guys. They'd come to me, thinking I could handle everything from repayment of loans to how they could get in touch with buddies stationed in England to why they weren't getting letters from their wives to helping them get married. One day I came back from my Uppingham bank trip to find that Miss Mason had taken a long distance call she couldn't handle. When I called back, it turned out to be from a field director some distance away, relaying a cable to a chap on our base. So I had to call him in and tell him his little ten-year-old brother had been drowned. That took a lot out of me. He cried first. Then I cried with him. We talked a long time, looking at snapshots of the little fellow and making arrangements for the man to send a cable home.

Another happening brought home the war in a poignant way. Most of the guys around the base wore raunchy fatigues and fatigue hats smashed down on their heads. They all looked pretty much alike—just a few hundred GIs. Then one day a chap came in to unload: seems his wife was not only stepping out on him but was arranging to sell their home back in Kentucky. He was hitting bottom, wondering what he could do when he honestly knew there was nothing at all to be done. He made me realize that inside each of those fatigues I saw around the base could be one often lonely, hurting human being. It made a great difference in how I saw the guys and saw my job.

British Tommy, the great piano player, was also an excellent dancer; he had actually been a dance instructor. So we started dancing classes for the guys. It was I who suffered. When we held dances and brought in truckloads of British girls as hostesses, all those beginners who didn't have the courage to ask the new girls would seek me out. I'd dance my legs off almost to the knees, it seemed, and had to shower off the brick-red paint that flaked off that concrete floor we'd so laboriously painted.

I'll never forget the first dance. From the time I got up in the morning till midnight I was going at top speed. Some of the guys came in to decorate, and of course someone needed something every minute—from ladders, wire, scissors, knives or paint for the bulbs to trucks for moving benches and piano, getting flowers, and the like. They made a whole false ceiling with camouflage nets (the heavy brown netting interwoven with brown and green burlap that they carry on all their trucks so they can take cover if necessary. Then they brought in boughs to cover the stoves, with ferns across the front of the stage. The place was transformed, especially with the dim lights coming from behind all the decorations. We had invited women from four different places, and I thought we were all set. Then one group telephoned they couldn't come. To replace that contingent, Miss Mason called a friend who rounded up a truckload of women from a village near here. At 6:30 I had a battery of drivers and convoy officers in my office briefing them on their trips. I got them all off, only to have a call from the motor pool half an hour later that one truck had broken down. I tried to call the little hotel where the gals were to be picked up but found it had no phone. Nevertheless, we finally, if somewhat late, ended up with a grand crowd of women—ATS (like our WACs), WAAFs (WAVEs), WLA (Land Army) and civilians—about 175 in all.

There was a great turnout of GIs. Then I started to sweat out the orchestra, which was to come from a base eight miles away. The dance was to start at 8:00 P.M., and at 8:30 I called the base and was told they had left at 6:45. I pictured them wandering around trying to find our base. While we waited, I tried to get two good pianists from the base but found they were both off on pass. So until the orchestra finally arrived, we played records over the public address system.

We had several dances while I was there and, now that I think of it, no casualities or accidents, no alcohol or drug episodes—a good record, I think, compared with young people today. The British military gals came in uniform, in which they seemed much at home. I always wanted to talk with them and compare notes from my experience in the WAAC, but being in charge of the whole show, I never found time to sit down. I deeply admired the British in another way too. When we had discussion groups at the club, not only were the Brits on base always there, but they were knowledgeable about history and world politics—including the States—whereas most of our GIs couldn't care less, even those few who'd show up. I kept wondering why.

On June 4, 1944, there was no time to wonder about anything but the rumors that filled the air. The base was sealed; GIs reported special guards at each gate; no one, but on one, was allowed on or off the base. And when a small contingent of our officers came to chow that evening under guard, our suspicions about some kind of military action seemed justified. We later learned that those officers had been briefed for the big D-Day landing. Paratroopers had been flown in for our C-47s to drop or carry over on gliders. When the operation was postponed because of weather, the 315th had to feed, entertain, and keep calm all those hundreds of extra men.

The next morning as I was walking into the club kitchen, I saw a GI snitching donuts from a tray on a counter. I smiled and said, "Hey, that's verboten!" Grinning back, he chomped on the donut, and started to talk. He turned out to be a Special Services sergeant from the paratroopers, let out of the fenced-in compound to arrange a movie for the guys. "I heard about your club and thought I'd check it out." We went to my office for a long talk. He gave me the American flag shoulder patch they'd been given to designate them as U.S. forces, saying, "I may not need this any more." And he gave me my first hand grenade. We went outside, took the powder out, and threw it over the brick wall to set off the cap. It was then safe as a great souvenir.

You can imagine our feelings as we watched all our C-47s take off on July 6, some towing gliders. Then, of course, we spent the day in a kind of hollow tension until we saw them—most of them—coming in on the home flight. As we waited, I'd thought, "This is something bomber bases go through much of the time." Here at the 315th the men had only been practicing, to be ready when needed. Much of the time one wondered whether there even *was* a war going on. Now we knew! And soon we learned more details about happenings on the Continent—of Hitler's invasions and atrocities, and of the determined underground of anti-Nazi clergy and high German officers who had tried unsuccessfully to stop the Nazi dictatorship by assassinating Hitler and were praying that we'd arrive in time to help. We were too late, of course; that very year more than twenty-five such conspirators were hanged or shot.

Meanwhile, we had our own duties at the club. Eventually, we no longer had to import dance bands; one was formed on our base, led by Larry Justin. He'd played with Hal Kemp's Orchestra, one of the great old big bands, whose theme song had been "Got a Date with an Angel." Larry played trumpet superbly. The crowd always begged for his rendition of "Stardust," and when he hit the closing high note, the crowd was all with him. And even though ours was an enlisted men's club, Lieutenant Larry loved to spend his spare time with us doing his arranging.

One time when the base was sealed for some military reason and we had to cancel a dance, Larry said he'd bring the band over anyway. He knew a chap who'd been an emcee in the states who could do a program for us. This was Lucky Evans. Though I must admit he was good, his "good" was the suggestive kind the guys loved. My social education was tested that evening. I was sitting in the crowd about halfway back. When Lucky would tell a dirty story, chaps in front would turn around to sneak a look and those behind me lean out to catch my expression. Heaven help me; I didn't know whether to join in and hoot with them, to be stiff and prissy, or try for something in between—which is what I think I did!

For the second overseas anniversary of the 315th Troop Carrier Group, there was a big celebration planned. Larry and Lucky were to go to London to book some professional entertainers and invited me to go along. We met another Red Cross girl Lucky knew in London, and the four of us went to theatrical agencies, where Larry and Lucky booked several acts—including striptease dancers and the works!

That evening Larry took us into a Picadilly lounge in the basement of a big hotel, where guys went to pick up elite "commandos," as they called them. Guys could choose from blondes, brunettes, and redheads. At one point Larry said, "Watch me. I'll show you how it's done." He went to sit by himself and enticed a striking blonde to his table. She plied her trade until Larry felt he'd provided enough show for us and gave her a brushoff. Then she was anything but a lady. The British lingo wasn't pretty, but I couldn't blame her. For a guy less picky, there were plenty of girls on the street. Larry and Lucky said, "Fall back a way and watch us." We hadn't gone very far when we could see how easily they could get picked up.

When the big anniversary day came, there was a dilemma. No one had wondered about a place big enough to hold all the men on base; the largest was the hut in which they showed movies, and that wouldn't do. Colonel Mac, who I'd always felt was an "officers' man," suggested showing it just for the officers, but Larry said, "The anniversary is for everyone. If the GIs can't see it, I'll cancel the whole show." He stood his ground against the Scot and got away with it. It finally turned out that our Red Cross snack bar was the biggest Quonset on the base, so that's where the show happened. Needless to say, it was packed, with guys sitting in the windows, perching on tables, and almost hanging from the rafters. In my report to headquarters on programming, I did not mention the strippers, twirling tittie tassles and all. This was the guys' party, and they deserved a high old time!

Whenever I went to London on business, I stayed at a special Red Cross house in Berkeley Square. This was during the era of buzz bombs, Germany's V-2 robot bombs, and since they were part of life in London, I wanted to know more about them. One of the guys at chow told me, "Vi, they're not really new. I just read an article that said the U.S. Navy had one in 1918 but vetoed mass production for some reason. But this German version, is a pretty ingenious deal. It's simple enought to be mass produced cause it used just air as the major fuel. Somehow they expand it with a gasoline explosion that kicks first against the heat of the motor and then against the air behind. Can you imagine, they said it could carry a one-ton warhead over 150 miles at a 9,000-foot ceiling in any kind of weather. A gyro keeps it going in a straight line from the launch pad. I don't know if these pads are set, but I don't think they can move them around." I didn't understand it all, but I know the Germans rained V-2s on London, sometimes sending over more than a hundred a day. Statistics showed that at least one person was killed for each bomb; some killed none, but others killed a great many. That was when they started evacuating women and children from London.

I still recall my first! As you heard that eerie faint whistle, you were supposed to run for the shelters, but we crazy Americans wanted first to see the bomb, looking like a tiny black plane. If the sound kept getting louder and louder, you knew it was headed in your direction, and you'd mentally urge it to keep going on beyond where you were; when the sound stopped, that even eerier silence meant that the bomb would drop straight down! I'd been out on a date that night and returned to the RC House in Berkeley Square to find hardly anyone around: "They're all up in Betty's room sweating out buzz bombs!" As I walked in, the only space left was on the bed if someone moved over. I joined them there, leaning against the headboard. The house did seem to be one of the corridors from set launch, for bombs had actually landed in a lake just beyond. So we had the full treatment of hearing two of them get louder and louder. When the engine would cut out, we'd all hold our breath—until we heard the explosion. Then we'd relax, let out a yell, and pass around a bottle of Scotch to fortify us for the next one!

Another time in London I was the guest of Rex, my Australian friend from the *Queen Mary*. He'd shown up unexpectedly at the club one day and made me promise I'd come to London. Rex got me special billets and took me to Madame Tussaud's Wax Works. It was spookingly real! That evening we were at the KODAK Club, their Aussie gathering place in London. I was entranced with uniforms and the accents. The guys were whooping it up when one bet another he couldn't drink a huge mug of beer without using his hands. He was on! So everyone gathered round, putting coins in the hat, as the challenged chap got down on the floor on his knees. With his hands behind his back, he lifted the heavy filled glass with his teeth, guzzling the beer as he tipped it ever higher, till it was empty. There was silence as we watched, but cheers broke out when he finished.

After my driver Jim, another Texan I'd give almost anything to track down today was George, one of the most unlikely of the RC commandos. I say unlikely, for he wasn't the kind you'd expect to hang around the house. Just the opposite. In my Minnesota upbringing, his personal code of ethics was something I'd not before encountered. I admired it in a strange kind of way, but it cost me some sleepless nights.

George drank too much; and because I felt he was somehow special, I was trying to do something about this. He'd often get into fights—usually, I was to learn, because of a matter of principle. How many times I cleaned and bound up his bloodied knuckles! The code I mentioned went something like this. "If you are my friend and straight, you know without doubt I'd lay down my life for you; but if you ever cross me, buddy, look out!" If George promised to do something, he'd do it if it killed him. Like the time he'd promised to hang parachutes for a dance—the color-coded chutes they used to identify what kind of supplies or equipment was being dropped. To lower and camouflage the high, bare ceilings of the Quonsets, we'd rope the center of the chutes up to the ceiling and then catch up the sides to make a most attractive, flowerlike false ceiling. To do it, we had to use long, long ladders. This time George came in looking gaunt and pale with a hangover. In ETO language, "I surely sweat him out that time!"

We didn't have a fireplace in the club, but sometimes after hours George and I would light a fire in a kitchen cookstove, then open the firebox door so we could see the flames. We'd sit in the dark with our feet propped up and talk for hours. I found that he had been adopted and had had good parents—

except that his dad wanted him to be able to lick all the kids on the block, and his mother had tried to dress him like a little Lord Fauntleroy. He'd found out that he had a sister and said, "After the war, Vi, one thing I'm going to do is find my real mom and my sister." I wonder if he ever did!

George was a tech sergeant in charge of one squadron's parachute department. Others told me how the guys loved him. He'd stick his neck out to let some who had married British girls, or had fathered kids in Birmingham or someplace, get off to see their families. But, as I said, let one of them take advantage or cross him in any way! All that aside, a thing I always wondered about was how George could always be so neatly dressed and well groomed. Perhaps his mother had had some influence after all!

On July 10 I had a call from London that a staff assistant would arrive the next day on the four o'clock train. Later I wrote home:

Spanhoe Airdrome, July 14, 1944

Virginia is a swell egg, taller than I am and rather quiet. She's from Nebraska, and even though she's worked for the Book of the Month Club in New York City the last four years, she still gives the impression of the modest, practical Midwest—not unattractive, but not a gal one would pick out of a crowd. We picked up stuff to furnish another room in our quarters and get Virginia settled, just before I had to take off for London. Jim drove me down.

The "buzzards" were horrible that night in London. Jim told me that in the wee hours the buzz bombs hit so close they blew out doors where he was staying, and plaster and glass were falling all around. Jim had a call to stay over another day. I had to get back so decided to take the train and went to the station an hour early, only to find a line of people four abreast and about a block and a half long waiting for my train: London evacuees.

7 Winter in Britain

When the summer was over and the cold, damp winter rolled in, we had new problems. A big one was how to heat the huge Quonsets with the "Limey" (British) stoves that came with them. They were cast iron, about three feet high, maybe eighteen inches wide, and less than a foot deep, with funny little grates. A line of them down the center of the long Quonset just didn't do the job, even though the army had given me a funny little GI to help keep them going. Jack was from Georgia and was to become an invaluable helper. We tried everything to start the coal-burning stoves, including rags on sticks dipped in kerosene. Even that didn't always work.

By that time, though, I'd found I could get almost anything from the supply officer by making a big nuisance of myself. So I talked him out of a whole bunch of potbelly stoves—those big, round, heavy cast-iron barrellike jobs. They did a far better job, even though we'd fry on one side and still be cold on the other.

We still had a small Limey stove in my office, and I have snapshots of some of us sitting around in parkas and boots to keep warm. I've often said that I've never been so cold as I was that winter in England. When visiting in British cottages, which were heated with little pots of coals in fireplaces, I'd keep on my woolen overcoat over my wool uniform.

In addition to the cold, with hundreds of GIs coming into the club out of snow or mud with grimy wet boots, our floors took a beating. Seeing it in the morning before it was scrubbed and cleaned up from the night before, could be pretty depressing. We didn't open till eleven in the morning but stayed open till eleven at night, when there were always those who would say, "Just let me finish this letter home to my wife."

One Sunday I truly hit bottom! As I mentioned, Colonel Mac could be funny, but he could be difficult. Even though he had said, "Anything Vi wants, she can have," this time I couldn't. And of course, being a Kochendoerfer and unable to deny my German background, I did at times display what is sometimes called "bullheadedness." It's particularly interesting now that I can't even remember what I was fighting for, only that it was something I thought was important, and I wanted it to happen right then and to happen my way. I hit a stone wall.

I was back in my chilly office that Sunday afternoon feeling truly sorry for Vi and stewing a long time. But then something happened! I relaxed and said to myself, "What the Hell, Vi. What if this whole Goddamned club has to close up. It wouldn't be a world calamity!" I seldom use swear words, and I can't remember now whether I said it out loud or to myself. Either way, it relieved the pressure, and everything worked out that next week.

I was to think of that experience many times over the years to come, realizing that we can be our own worst enemies. When the bottom fell out of my little world (as it did several times in my three and a half years overseas), I could say to myself, "Vi, a couple of weeks, a month, a year from now, you'll look back on this and say, 'Why did I ever get so upset?'" I learned that most things were never as bad as they seemed at that particular moment; if I didn't take myself or my job or project too seriously, it would work out OK, and sometimes even beyond the best I could imagine. I was reminded of what an aunt of mine used to say, "Let go and let God." This experience helped me create my own version, "You can't *make* things happen, but you can *let* them, by taking yourself out of the way." It also reminded me of words of a good friend, "Vi, you can't make the world over, overnight!"

One day a sergeant from base headquarters came by the office. "I'm to pick you up and take you to see the MP sergeant." I couldn't imagine why but dropped what I was doing and climbed into the jeep. As I stood before the sergeant's desk, he said, "This is embarrassing, Miss Kochendoerfer, but did you forge a signature on a paycheck for PFC Larson?" I thought for a moment, and then, "Oh yes, but that was weeks and weeks ago."

"But did you realize what you were doing?"

"Well, Carl often helped around the club. He came in with a check—an allotment check—which had been made out to his wife. He said, 'She always sends it back to me, but this time she forgot to endorse it. Will you endorse it for me, Vi?'"

"Didn't you realize what you were doing?"

"Well—I did point out to Jim that this would be illegal. He said, 'But Vi, haven't I helped you out lots of times around here?' So I signed the check with his wife's signature."

The sarge then pointed out the legal consequences of what I'd done and went on to say, "this time you may not have to appear at a court martial with Larson, but I do want you to know that what you did was so serious that I hope you never do it again, no matter how much they beg."

On top of that, a week later—after not having been able to get to the bank for a week—I was checking the cash and found that all the bills were gone—84 pounds, $342! The money had been taken from the cigar box I had hidden on a shelf in the closet in our quarters. And this was the second time! The field director just happened to come by that day, so we got the provost marshal and tried to find clues. Nothing came to light. I reported it and realized I'd hear from the Red Cross commissioner and that there might even be an investigation. But I felt I'd done the best I could, and angrily blamed headquarters for not providing some kind of safe.

One Sunday morning as I came into the club, little Georgia Jack, who built the fires, was waiting. "I've come to say good-bye, Miss Vi. I'm leaving on D.S. [detached service] at noon today." Well, after just having gotten things perking with several personnel shifts, this seemed the last straw. Jack practically ran the place for me: he unlocked the club at eight in the morning when the help arrived, built fires when needed, did all the odd jobs, made all the coffee in the evening, kept records on the Coca-Cola shipments, and dispatched the trucks and details to pick up supplies. He never took time off and was there from eight in the morning till ten-thirty or later at night.

Now he kissed all the cooks goodbye, and I actually shed tears when he said, "I've never hated leaving any place as much as this, Miss Vi." After he left, I tracked down his commanding officer and told him we couldn't run our club without Jack, plus other sob stuff. His captain, a good egg, said, "They had to send someone, and Jack seemed the most likely. But I'll see what I can do about a replacement. Call you about one."

I waited and sweated out that call, and by three o'clock I had given up. About fifteen minutes later Jack came bouncing in as only he could: "they sent someone else!" We hugged each other! Now, in watching reruns of M.A.S.H., I deeply love Radar because he reminds me of Jack, who'd do anything to help and so quietly kept his part of things running smoothly. They even looked a bit alike!

So that situation worked out. But then I had a real confrontation with the brass—something to write home about!

Spanhoe Airdrome, October 28, 1944

I need to unload! First off, Virginia has been transfered, so I'm here alone once again. That I could take, since I'd done it before she came. But I've had a real feud with Special Services. It started with our own show here at the club. SS really should put on such things, but never did. So I went to Larry, my Hal Kemp lieutenant. He and Lucky Evans and I cooked up a great show with the band. It was the talk of the base. The SS captain came but wouldn't even help get the footlights connected when we asked him, yet he brought the colonel and tried to take over, like telling me when to dim the house lights and such.

The colonel thought it would be a great idea to have a show a week. I told him that was too often. Then Friday of the next week the Special Services captain came over to me in the mess hall. Most of the others had left, and Ginny and I had been talking to two chaps sitting across the table from us. The captain looked down at me and said, "I have a proposition to make. I'm not sure how you'll take it, but we've decided to put the enlisted men's movies on in your club." The smirk on his face was sickening.

"That's all very nice, except it just isn't possible."

"What do you mean? If we want to, we jolly well can."

"Well, I have something to say about this, and the answer is 'no!'" He bristled at that.

"If Colonel Mac wants this, he's the commander of this base, and he'll do it."

"If you'd have troubled to ask, you'd have found that it's against the colonel's agreement with Red Cross and so against base policy. I'm in charge of what happens in our buildings; and if you feel you have to have them, let me know, and I'll arrange for us to move out." The volume of our voices kept building.

"You seem to know little about Army channels."

"I haven't been *in* the Army eight months for nothing."

And then the payoff: "Well, then, you're either too stupid or too ignorant to understand what's going on."

At that point I stood up, glared at him, and said, "that I don't have to take from anyone—least of all from an officer, who's supposed to be a gentleman, if for no other reason than by act of Congress."

I saw the look of "touché" in the eyes of the two officers and went on to explain that what he wanted to do meant we couldn't have any program of our own, and we'd have to close the snack bar.

"Well, as far as I'm concerned," he countered, "anything you do isn't very important anyway."

"I've always thought that's what you felt, but it's good to hear it face to face. No matter what you think of our program, it's far more than you're doing. You and the colonel take pretty good care of the officers, but I feel I need to fight for the GIs."

I was so angry at this point that I started to cry, and at that he left.

Next day I went to see Captain Fry, the adjutant, who's a pretty good egg except that I feel he takes too much from the colonel. "I want to tell you what happened last night before you get the other side." I told him of the encounter and went on, "I don't mind that Special Services doesn't help at all, but when they start fighting us, it's time to have some kind of understanding."

I guess there were so many gripes against the SS captain that he did get talked to; at any rate, little by little, in a sort of sheepish way, he seems to be coming around. At a big dinner for a visiting general some time later, he was feeling plenty good and reached over with a cigar: "Here, Miss Kay, have one on me." So I took it, smiled, and said, "Peace pipe, Captain?" His sergeant said next morning the captain told him, "Miss Kay and I have buried the hatchet," and Ed had answered to himself, "Yeh, how far?" But things are on an even keel again, which is a good feeling.

We haven't even celebrated Thankgiving, but already the fellows are getting restless. Christmas is going to be a hard time for them, and we'll have a big job to do. Not that I haven't been thinking of the States myself—football games, Thanksgiving, and Christmas coming up. The mess halls took care of the turkey and trimmings, and we initiated the British gals into our Thanksgiving with a big dance and a great program.

Larry's band is getting really smooth. We had almost two hundred women, and everyone was in a lively mood. The band had us doing rhumbas, congas, tangos, and things you wouldn't understand—typically British—like the hokey-pokey and the polly glide. And afterward, back in my office, our special gang shared stuff that had been sent to them for Thanksgiving. We've been eating nuts, maple sugar, and even a can of ripe olives that appeared on my desk after I'd once mentioned how much I liked them.

❦

Shortly after I wrote that letter, circumstances developed that helped make the decisions for Christmas 1944. A big fat envelope was delivered to me marked TOP SECRET. I opened it gingerly to read that our 315th Group was to be moved to the Continent on a certain date and that we were to accompany them. I was told how many pounds of equipment and supplies I could send by air, how much by sea and so on, and ordered to begin making arrangements. I immediately went to see the supply officer to get material for crating and packing. It was difficult to handle this without being able to answer the many questions that came up.

After several days of hectic rushing around and wondering how we'd meet the deadline, another top-secret communication arrived saying the move had been canceled but that in January I was to be transferred to a Red Cross Club operating on a base not far from London. I was flown down to check things out, interview staff to see which members I'd like to keep, and such.

As it turned out, that transfer never happened, but of course I didn't know that as I spent the return trip stewing again about the powers that be, especially those at our headquarters. Here I'd just opened a club and gotten to know the men. Christmas was upon us—the loneliest time of the year for men who couldn't be home with parents and wives and children. The very reason for being here was to care about them. "Well," I thought, "I can do something about that!" So I called London and asked whether we could convert from a donut dugout to an aeroclub, which would allow us to serve a greater variety of food. I was thrilled to death to get the OK. But later, as I sat in the office to think about what I'd done, I began to wonder. I was to learn the hard way once again.

The next day there was a phone call from headquarters to pick up a new staff assistant to replace Virginia. It all happened overnight. The exact opposite of tall, slender, rather proper Ginny, Sue was short and cute, and one had the feeling she'd not be as committed to the job. At this particular time, training her was almost more of a problem than doing the big job of transition alone. I'm sure this says something about me, but right then I was frazzled myself and didn't need someone else to worry about.

Because food was rationed in England, as elsewhere, during the war, in order to get anything I had first to get a statement from the commanding officer as to the strength of the base so they could figure out how much to allow us. Then I had to find places to buy things like Spam and sardines and onions and buns and catsup and mustard so that we could make spamburgers and sardine sandwiches and such. And the staff had to be trained, charges decided on and budgeted.

This involved spending money over and above my thousand-pound revolving fund, which I had to reconcile each month in pounds, shillings, and pence. And if you try to reconcile your checking account each month, you know how you can spend minutes, hours, or even give up trying to make things balance. At any rate, when I reported to headquarters that my fund was running low, they just sent me a second thousand pounds to have to account for, bringing that responsibility to over $8,000!

After it was all over, however, I had time to share with family and friends the rest of my first Christmas overseas.

Christmas in England, Spanhoe Airdrome, December 30, 1944

We have a new Special Services officer! When I told him I'd need help, I got a committee from each squadron, and we went to work. Making Quonset huts look Christmasy isn't easy, but they really did! I took a detail of five men in a six-by (a two-and-a-half-ton truck) to a nearby estate, where we loaded up with holly, yew, and ivy. Two fourteen-foot trees came from another estate, and the kids from a village near here gave us a third. The guys rigged up tree lights, and we decorated with chaff—the tinfoil strips they toss out of planes to mess up the enemy's radar.

A stateside florist made holly and ivy ropes which draped each window group, with holly and mistletoe ropes falling down the center. Foot-high modernistic red letters down one side of the room read MERRY CHRISTMAS (which has now been changed to HAPPY NEW YEAR!) with an eight-foot wreath and huge bells at the top. I was darned proud of the job we did.

The first event of the holiday season was something we hadn't planned. On our way to the bank at Uppingham, Jim and I had stopped to invite fifty kids from Harringworth School near here. Once inside we got roped into giving a lecture on America to the whole school. We loved it when they got to asking questions: "What are gangsters like?" "What do American kids' faces look like?" "How big is America?" But then they asked to put on their nativity play for our GIs, and I said OK, thinking there'd be ten or so involved. Surprise! The whole school was in it, so they all came, plus the teachers and the vicar. The play was corny, and the guys loved it. Our GIs had a marvelous time feeding the tykes several Cokes apiece and stuffing their pockets with doughnuts.

The big event was the party we gave on the day before Christmas. I knew what our men would miss most was their own children, so we had invited two hundred kids (fifty from each of four schools) and arranged to have them picked up in Army trucks. The week before, we wrapped gifts from what GIs had donated out of their weekly rations. There were mountains of stuff. Each kid was to get about four candy bars, gum, a box of hard candy, Lifesavers, two packages of cookies, and miscellaneous other goodies.

The children were picked up in trucks and got here at one o'clock, all in their Sunday best. Though we thought we had a system for checking coats and boots, with two hundred kids any kind of organization just fell apart; we'd have to worry about that later. As the kids came in, each GI got one or more as his "family." An engineering group had saved nearly four pounds in British pennies (which look like copper quarters), some hapennies and sixpences, even a few half-crowns. We hid them all over the place and later had a penny hunt.

Lucky Evans ran the whole thing from behind the scenes. They didn't see him, but over the speakers came the voice of Father Christmas (Santa Claus to us): "Now later on I'm going to give you presents and then you'll see me. But all afternoon, even though you can't see me, I'll be watching you. If I see a little boy pulling a little girls' hair, or something like that, I'll remember it." The kids were wide-eyed and mystified. This was fun, even if it wasn't the best psychology. We played musical chairs too. Most men were possessive about "their" kids. How they wanted them to win! Then some of the kids sang for us and we loved it.

About that time I got a call from the MP at one of the gates: "Vi, what am I going to do? I've got fifteen or twenty kids here who've walked in all the way from Uppingham— about eight kilometers!" I didn't quite know what to do and didn't want to take responsibility for them. Finally I found some leftover candy and stuff that we could quickly gift-wrap, asked for a six-by and a driver, picked up the kids, and took them to the square in Uppingham. As we gave each a gift, we wished them a Merry Christmas and sent them home.

Got back just in time for refreshments. We'd gotten to-gether peanut butter-and-jam sandwiches and plain cake, plus two big fancy ones—one about three feet long and two feet wide, five layers high with all sorts of fillings, fla-vors, and decorations. There was cocoa, lemonade, orange and pineapple juice. Only the ice cream was missing; we had gotten all the ingredients ready and taken the mix to be frozen, only to find that the freezing plant in Upping-ham had broken down.

But the kids didn't know that, and they were entranced with the fruit juice. Some who had never tasted it before would take a sip and hold up the line as their faces lit up in wonder. And did they stuff—or, I sould say, did the GIs stuff the kids. Then we had to find everyone's coat and boots! Now Father Christmas stood in front of the big tree in the lounge, and the children filed around, each got two gifts. I can still see those happy tykes as we loaded them into the lorries (that's what they call our trucks).

I treasure the thank-you letters I received from Dudding-
ton School. I could see the teacher writing on the black-
board the way they were to begin: "Dear Friends from
America." The one I prized was from "Peter Sanders, Age
8." He forgot the "r" in "friends." I also had a letter from
one of the teachers: "On behalf of the children of Harringworth School I should like to thank you and your helpers
and all the foster fathers for Sunday's most enjoyable party.
I am sure that when you have returned safely to your
homes the children will all retain very happy memories of
the generosity and kindness of their American friends."

It was about five when we had them all loaded in
trucks, and our new snack bar was to open at seven. Sue
and I started to head for chow, but it was Christmas Eve,
and all the fellows wanted to buy us drinks. We relaxed
and joined the celebration for a while; then I excused myself to go eat, reminding Sue, "The snack bar opens at
seven." She promised she'd be along pronto: "Bill wants
to buy me one more drink." "You know I'll have enough
to do to get the snack bar under control," I cautioned her.
"You'll have to handle the program."

We opened the snack bar promptly at seven, much to
the delight of the guys who'd been waiting for the day
and made loving wisecracks about our innovations to sup-
plement the donuts with spamburgers and so on. A half-
hour passed, but no Sue. I was worn out and furious.
Feeling quite the martyr, I went to the library—a medium-
sized Quonset set at right angles to the big snack bar and
connected by an entryway—and started to play a Ronald
Coleman recording of Dickens's *Christmas Carol*. The place
was jammed, with standing room only, and we were all
quietly listening. I was the record changer for the stack of
78s.

At one point the door opened across the sea of heads.
There stood our new redheaded Special Services captain
and Colonel Mac. I nodded to them and went on listening. They left. A bit later the door opened again. It was
the Special Services officer alone. He motioned for me to

come. I wondered what could be important enough for me to push into that packed crowd, but I asked one fellow to change records and waded through. "Vi," he said, "the colonel was highly browned off that you didn't stop what you were doing and come speak to him after he'd gone out of his way to come to the club."

This was the spark that exploded the "cool" I'd tried to maintain during those past weeks of worry and work and planning and tension. I broke down in tears. I'd learned from earlier experience that most men don't know what to do with a tearful woman. I surely was glad we had a new SS officer, one I felt I could talk to, and that we were compadres rather than enemies. I started pouring out my feelings, and we ended up taking a walk down a snow-covered road. As we turned back, I said, "Take me to the quarters so I can wash my face before I go back to the club."

As we rounded the corner of the building, here was Sue weaving in. She took one look at me, and by the time I'd redone my face and returned to the club, Sue was there leading a big bunch of GIs in Christmas carols. I forgave her. I had a date with George to go to midnight mass, even though neither of us was Catholic. Much later, when I finally relaxed in bed, I felt we'd truly shown the guys and kids a good Christmas.

❧

After the holidays, things got back to a kind of normality. We had a great corps of women volunteers, headed by seventy-year-old Mrs. Kant, and her daughter Mary from the village of Harringworth. They biked in regularly to mend clothes or sew on butttons and insignia for the men, and were willing to do almost anything for us.

I often thought about the British women. We all knew guys on base who had women and even children in towns and cities like not-too-far-away Birmingham. Later the statistics of American-fathered children were staggering. Most of the men involved had families back home, but they were separated for months and years, with time on their hands, no one to care, sometimes wondering whether the next military raid might be their last. Then there were the mature British women whose notably undemonstrative husbands were also away fighting the war. It's not hard to understand how they could be swept off their feet by the lines of the American GI, or by gifts of chocolate, nylons, or who knows what? It must have been an undreamed-of world for some. Each man or woman was living in an artificial world, fulfilling a vital, instinctive, mutual need. Who was to judge?

All this came graphically home when, having tea with a family in the village, I was asked about the rumor that our assistant manageress—a married woman with a family, and one of our most trusted workers—was pregnant and that the father was a married man on base. At least I was prepared when the manageress herself told me about it two days later. When the story got around, the woman herself recognized that all I needed was more personnel problems, and offered to resign. She said, "I'll stay on till you can find a replacement." I hated to see her go but hired another woman who joined us the next month.

For our new menu, we experimented with the mostly canned rations, finding that fresh onions added a lot to mixtures of Spam or cheese or sardines. But it reminded me of a poem that captured "England" for many GIs—and even at times for me:

> Where the heavenly dew whips through the breeze,
> Where the sun don't shine and the rain flows free,
> And the fog is so thick you can hardly see,
>   That's England!
>
> Where you live on brussel sprouts and Spam,
> And powdered eggs not worth a damn,
> In town when you get fish and spuds,
> And down the taste with a jug of suds,
>   That's England!
>
> You hold your nose, when you gulp it down,
> It hits your stomach and makes you frown,

It burns your tongue, and your throat feels queer,
It's rightly named "bitter", it sure ain't beer,
    That's England!

Those pitch-black nights when you stay out late,
It's so bloody dark you can't navigate,
There's no transportation, so you have to hike,
And get smacked in the ass by a bloke on a bike,
    That's England!

It's only an island, around it's the drink,
Cut the balloons and let the damned thing sink.
I ain't complaining, but I'll have you know,
Life's rougher than Hell in the ETO.

On February 15, 1945, we were chatting over dessert when the phone rang. "It's for you, Vi. London calling." It was one of those scratchy calls that make it hard to hear anything, but finally I understood that it was someone at headquarters. Through the interference and garble, I made out, "You're being sent to the Continent . . ." Then, with difficulty and repetition, I learned that I was to report to London headquarters at ten o'clock Monday morning with all my belongings. This was Thursday. I remember saying (was it over the phone or to myself?), "But I don't want to go to France!"

I couldn't eat another thing. Sue seemed even more floored than I was with the thought of running the club by herself. When I told the colonel, he said if I wanted to stay he'd call London and see what he could do to keep me, but I decided it probably wouldn't do any good. Nice of him to offer though; he had truly mellowed toward us over the past months.

I started getting my stuff together. The goodbyes got to me a couple of times. Andy would play the piano and a whole gang would sing stuff especially for me. After a squadron dance, George and I sat up talking till early morning. One night Tiny (who weighed over two hundred pounds) called me to the table. I knew that the ordnance guys, with time on their hands, made lovely bracelets for their wives and girl-friends out of the stainless steel firewall of a C-47. The bracelets were handsome—a wide band with a big shiny buckle.

They'd often brought them in for me to try on for size. That evening Tiny was spokesman for a group, and with a corny little speech he handed me a package. I opened it to find a 315th TC bracelet, which I treasure and wear to this day. It's a unique conversation piece.

My favorite squadron arranged a program for the night before I was to leave. The guys said all sorts of silly and wonderful things to me over the mike. Later that night Sue had a little private party for four of our special friends and the two of us. She'd wrangled a quart of Scotch from the officers' club for the occasion, even though they don't allow off-sales, and George brought a big can of beer from the pub. Miss Mason had left a beautiful tray of tuna sandwiches and pastries with creamed crab cakes from stuff Sue and I had gotten in the mail from home. We drank and ate and reminisced till late. George stayed a while after that, and it was twenty minutes to seven next morning when I got to my quarters.

I was supposed to be in London by ten that morning, so I got only an hour's sleep. The colonel had said we could have a staff car to take all my stuff, and I'd requested Jim (my first love there—on his side, not mine) as my driver. I'd asked him to come at nine. That was in itself a bit of rebellion, since London was at least a three-hour drive. We finally set off at ten, and I reported in four hours late. Even so, I finished clearing that afternoon, since I'd already gotten physicals, pictures, and fingerprints when I was to have moved but didn't. I did get new noncombative identification, dog tags checked, lots of new clothes and equipment such as battle dress (pants, short Eisenhower jacket, billed hat) and warm underwear. "Wonderful," I thought, "now that we're leaving England, where I've frozen more than anywhere in my life!" Then I heard that Paris and much of France had no heat at all.

There was a kind of "gone" feeling in the prospect of starting all over again from scratch. I though about my friends at Spanhoe, and all the ups and downs and damned hard work that had gone into building up that club. But it was also the dawning of a recognition—gained from the repeated experi-

ence of having to start over again—that there was something
that needed doing wherever I was to go, and that in a matter
of weeks I'd find more new friends and a new home away
from home. In a way, too, I was glad to be getting to the
Continent, where the real action seemed to be happening.

Thinking of that brought back the old adventuresome
wondering what it would all bring! What would it be like to
be in France not speaking French? Maybe I should have
asked to be shipped straight to Germany; I'd had a semester
of German at Reed College and had learned from Granny
Kochendoerfer to *sprechen* a *kleine bischen deutsch.*

I had another week in London, and George pulled strings
to get a two-day pass to spend with me. We did sightseeing,
saw Alfred Lunt and Lynn Fontanne in a marvelous play,
had dinner, and visited two of his special pubs. He was a
sweet guy who'd taught me a lot about human values in a
somewhat foreign but unforgettable way, and he would re-
main a touchstone in my later life.

PART III

With the Airborne from Paris to Berlin

8 Paris in the Spring

I still treasure "the first time I saw Paris" in the spring! Right off it seemed to top anything I'd seen or done in England. Compared to the dark, damp drabness of London, Paris seemed on wings with its wide boulevards, its light, airy architecture, and the sunny blue sky. I had an assignment to leave the following Monday morning to set up a club for the 17th Airborne Division at Châlons-sur-Marne, about 150 kilometers east of Paris.

Meanwhile, I found my Washington friend Smitty again. She was waiting assignment too, and we joined in exploring and going to spring fashion openings at Maggie Rouffs, Lucien LeLongs, and Mad Carpentiers. We did Concord Square, dodged the wild taxis whose drivers seem to live by the horn, had tea at the Ritz, and learned how to get around on the Metro—the underground that epitomized Paris during the war for me. Metro cars were utterly jammed. Once in, you questioned whether to breath, as the life-giving air was a pungent puree of B.O., French perfume, and garlic!

We went to the Paris Opera with some officers we'd met. That night I learned how to tip: the ushers who seated us, the woman in the washroom. Before I excused myself to patronize that spot, my date reached into his pocket and handed me something in an upside-down fist: "You'll need this." It was a tiny flat pack of tan K-ration toilet paper, which he knew I wouldn't find in the rest room, regardless of tips.

I learned from my date that the next night was something special—the opening of the Paris Stage Door Canteen. He was on duty and couldn't go, but Smitty and I did.

It was great evening. We sat at tables where we could order drinks and were joined by two chaps who were on the staff of *Yank*, the official military magazine. Smitty's friend was George; mine was Art. They bought us drinks, and we checked the program in awe: in person—Noel Coward, Marlene Dietrich, Maurice Chavelier! Noel Coward was a privilege to see and hear in an informal setting. Marlene sang encore upon encore with her famous "Lili Marlene." Chevalier was the greatest! After the show we talked with him, and when he found out that Smitty's name was Louise, he sang "Louise" for us, while a GI taped it for Smitty.

How many times those days the thought had gone through my mind, "Wouldn't it be great to have a jeep to drive around Paris!" When I mentioned I'd love to got to the flea market, Art said, "We can promote a jeep. Where can we pick you up in the morning?" It was Sunday. We drove to the flea market in Place Pigalle, where they sold everything from grand pianos to safety pins at stands on the street.

We drove around Montmarre, and climbed steep curvy roads to the famed Sacre Coeur, and had a breathtaking view of Paris spread out before us. We lunched at their Allied Expeditionary Forces Club in the Grand Hotel. Then we did the races at Longchamps, stopping afterward at our American Red Cross mess hall, La Potinnier, which we called "The Pot."

I had another day with Art before leaving. We did the sights in daylight and that last evening strolled down the Champs-Elysées, stopping at sidewalk cafes. Then Art had an idea for celebrating this special evening. He knew a secret spot where, after a special rap on the door and a bit of bargaining in French, a bottle of champagne would change hands.

We walked to Art's hotel. He felt it would be more comfortable to go up to his room to celebrate. I balked at this: "It isn't just Vi K. going up to your room with you, it's a Red Cross gal in uniform." Art grinned. "Vi, who are you worried about? This is France! That desk clerk would perhaps be more surprised if he knew nothing might happen up there than if it did." So he talked me into it, and we had a long, memorable exchange, mostly hanging out of the window and drinking champagne as we watched the moving scene on the Champs-Elysées.

I left Paris the next day, and a week later I had a letter
from Art on *Yank* Continental Edition letterhead, suggesting
things we could do next time I came to Paris, and closing
with "Love (I like it that way)." I wrote home about my first
French assignment.

Châlons-sur-Marne, France, April 15, 1945

I'm here with 17th Airborne! The name means Châlons
on the banks of the Marne River, a city of about 30,000 in
northeastern France. I was to open a club, and left Paris
with a French driver and all my stuff and basic equipment
jammed into a weapons carrier and trailer—like a couple
of gypsies traveling with all our worldly belongings. At
least three times we heard a clatter and bang and had to
pull over and walk back to pick up pails and supplies off
the highway.

It was terribly cold. We stopped at a little restaurant the
French driver knew to get warm by a kitchen fire. They said
they could feed us, so we sat down. A little boy about ten,
who felt proud he knew a few "American" words, brought
a hot brick for each of us to warm our feet. Then the meal
started. First, cold meats with French bread and wine.
Then two fried eggs apiece, followed by hot pastries with
meat filling, and then veal roast and French fries and more
wine. It just kept coming in that funny way the French
have of serving everything separately. Cream cheese and
apple pie with coffee topped it all off. The coffee was pretty horrible, but the food was great and warm.

The welcome at Châlons was in grand style. They'd
found billets for me in a private home which, glory be, had
a water heater, compliments of the Germans who'd been
earlier tenants and demanded all the comforts of home. So
I'll have the luxury of hot showers, which I understand are
pretty scarce.

We weren't to be here very long, so instead of requisi-
tioning buildings the Army got a huge yellow and white
striped tent about eighty feet long for a temporary setup.

It's like a circus tent, except they set it up in a muddy field.
While waiting for all this to happen, I went back to Paris
with a truck to pick up donut supplies and more stuff we
needed.

The roads in France were a welcome relief after the narrow, winding ones of England, though not as picturesque—
or as comfortable. In spots where they were nothing but
potholes from bombings and frost blisters, they really in-
flicted punishment during a long trip in a truck or a jeep
that had no springs or warm upholstery.

By the time I returned they had installed lights in the
tent and brought in a radio. The plan was to pick up the
whole tent and move it from week to week to serve different areas of the division. All this sounds pretty makeshift,
but actually we found we were servicing about six or seven
times as many men as we had at the expansive spread at
Spanhoe. And you can't imagine how nice a tent can be.
The guys thought it was great.

Already I was comparing them with the 315th. I know I
bragged about them a lot, but the 17th Airborne guys
seemed ten times as appreciative, largely because they'd
never had much, I guess. A few remarks: "Golly, just to
have a back on the chair to lean on." "Can't seem to write a
letter with so much light." "Gee, just to relax and listen to
that music," or "Just to talk with a gal who speaks English!" They set up a little tent for us with cots to rest on,
and a separate one with a two-holer john, which sported a
sign made by one of the GIs: Off Limits to Army Personal.

❧

The French family I lived with was great. I learned that they'd
been put out of part of their home by the Germans for four
years (our army could requisition only those houses the Germans had used); on the door of my room were four German
names of former occupants, three of them crossed out. The
room had two large windows with wide sills, overlooking a
walled garden in which the trees were already spring-dressed

in pink and white. I found I had not only hot water—which took a couple of hours to heat with electricity—but also the one bathtub in town.

On opening day in the big tent we were confronted with the question of where to get water for coffee; there was no spigot to turn on! We hit the mess halls and got field ranges set up to boil water in thirty-gallon GI cans. On the whole, the division was willing to do anything for us. Seemed they'd been through a lot with few creature comforts. I had a permanent detail of eight GIs and their sergeant—a grand crew! I remember best Bud, Pep, and Hal. Hal was a tall, slender blond with big blue eyes. It was his idea that if I was going to work with the Airborne, best I knew how to protect myself; in his book, some commando tactics were in order! We had a workout each day and I learned how not to get thrown as I was the first time! I learned a bit of pidgin French too, since I had what was called there a "frog staff" at the club. So there were *combien* ["how much?" which we were to use a lot, later on] and *mercy butter-cups* and *silver plates*.

Mail finally caught up with me, including an envelope of stuff that had accumulated in England, so a long letter home was in order. I wrote several pages about Paris exploits with Art when I'd be there overnight on business, and tried to explain George and other boyfriends in Britain to Mom, who, given her background, was ever seeing matrimony in the picture.

I commiserated with the cigarette situation in the States and said I wished I could send them some, since I got mine for pennies. The French would pay us up to 150 francs (three dollars) for a pack, and cigarettes were good for tips. I hadn't as yet tried to buy anything with them, though we had gotten a dozen fresh eggs at a farmhouse one day in exchange for a couple of bars of soap.

I was still exploring Châlons and working to get the club going when almost overnight the whole division took off on one of the last expeditions of World War II. With just a handful of guys left in the rear, there was hardly anything to do. We kept the tent club open at headquarters of the 17th and took donuts and huge urns of coffee to outlying groups on a trailer attached to a motor bike. It was dangerous driving on potholed roads. On days off I had a trip to Rheims, the champagne spot, and was disappointed that we couldn't get inside the grand cathedral there. Even all boarded up, it was impressive in a way no church I'd seen in the States could ever be.

One evening we were sharing a bottle of champagne in one of the tents when an officer came by in a German convertible. He was just back from the front, and we sat spellbound for an hour listening to his tales. Now I knew I was close to the war. In a way I was glad I hadn't as yet gotten to know a lot of fellows well; many of them wouldn't be coming back. I quietly cringed when I'd hear "So and so, and so and so, got it." One evening several men had an eight-by-ten glossy of their company; they'd point to the dead and share some of their innermost thoughts about how they felt to be survivors.

Hal, my favorite blue-eyed blond, had gone up with a supply contingent and came back with some German cognac that was really smooth. "We captured the factory, and after that we didn't drink water any more. In fact, we even filled the water tanks with it," he told us. I myself could easily have gotten to be a toper on cognac, armagnac, calvados, vodka, and of course champagne, which was getting to be quite common. We often had champagne, wine, or beer at the mess hall; it wasn't on the menu, but someone would bring it in. Besides liquor, the guys came back with the darnedest things. One evening a chap walked in wearing a Jerry officer's cap, saluted and yelled, "Heil!" Another had brought back a Steinway grand with the legs cut off.

I'm not sure just who or why, but there were a lot of German prisoners around doing all sorts of menial jobs such as mopping floors in the hospital. They were good workers; I thought maybe they were darned glad to be out of combat and offered clean clothes and food. To see the stuff the French wore on their feet often made my own feet hurt. Some had nothing more than cloth slippers. There were sandals of all kinds—one wondered how they kept them on—and thick-wooden-soled creations that looked something like ski boots. With but a handful of 17th men left in the rear, we had no need for the huge tent at Headquarters. One day as we had just finished taking it down a Red Cross supervisor drove up in a little British Hillman. "I'm looking for a Vi Kochendoerfer." "You've found her," I replied. She had the special job of trying to keep in touch with women assigned to airborne divisions, because we moved around so much.

"There's little to do here in Châlons," I told her. "If I don't get another assignment, I think I'll take off and see some of the country." After thinking a while, she said, "Well, would you like to go to West Germany and set up a donut operation with the forward echelon of the 82d Airborne?" Of course I would! She gave me an hour or so to pack my worldly belongings once again, and this April of 1945 I was off on another adventure. The French driver helped load my things in the Hillman, which looked like a miniature truck. As we drove away, the supervisor said, "They keep moving, so I'm not sure just where 82d is now, but we'll find them."

9 German Surrender and Meeting the Russians

Echternach! That's where the ruins of war first hit me! No standing buildings—just mounds of brick and mortar that had once been a little German town! My supervisor and I were all eyes as our French driver eased along a single lane cleared just wide enough for a jeep to get through. There was more of the same in Metz and Verdun.

After an overnight in historic Luxembourg—the lovely capital city of the tiny Grand Duchy tucked in between France, Germany, and Belgium and built around a tenth-century castle—we drove through some of the desolation left by the Battle of the Bulge, quite regularly inquiring at military road blocks about the location of the 82d Airborne. Finally, late in the afternoon, we hit the jackpot at a road block where the guards said, "We're 82d! The division is up ahead around Cologne. You just take this road . . ."

Cologne, Germany, Friday, April 27, 1945

I'm in the living room of a nice home with fire in the fireplace, radio playing, fresh red tulips on the table, wine to sip. I have an ARC compadre—Evelyn Stevens; we call her Stevie.

Not much left of the University, or of the center of the City of Cologne, which must have been beautiful at one time. It's a miracle, though, that the slim, lacy twin spires of the cathedral, though scarred, still stand like sentinels. That must have taken some precision bombing, for almost everything around it is flat with piles of rubble.

This section of Cologne has lovely large houses, people are well dressed and don't seem to be hurting for a thing. We have plenty of coal, electric stove, etc. Flowers are beautiful.

Stevie and I spent a grand week in that luxurious apartment in suburban Cologne, but we had just gotten the donut kitchen operating when the division got orders to move forward into combat. What followed was a period of hectic activity— during which *the war in Europe ended*—and six weeks passed before I had time to write home again. My long recital of those unforgettable experiences was taken largely from my journal.

Sissone, France, Tuesday, June 12, 1945

Well, after a perfectly hectic day of again closing clubs and loading trains (this time to Epinal, France) I'm going to get started on a news that will probably end up a book. It will start when I last wrote way back in April in Cologne. So many unbelievable things have happened, I want to get it all together on paper.

When the 82d took off and again we were left with a small group in the rear, Stevie and I started haunting the C.P. (command post, or 82d Headquarters). We wanted to join the action, and finally General Swift (of three commanding generals, the one who was left in the rear) gave in. He issued orders that we were to go back with General Gavin's C-47 when it arrived.

We took off two days later with the two pilots and the crew chief. Stevie and I were the only passengers and had the generals' big, soft upholstered seats up front on each side. I had my nose plastered to the window to see the beautiful wooded countryside, some still snow-covered. In places trees had been felled to leave a clearing in the woods in the shape of a big letter, which I learned later was a signal to German planes.

It was a seven-hundred-mile trip. We let down at a large airport at Braunschweig (Brunswick) to refuel, and as we taxied to a stop, a big military sedan pulled up. Out jumped a chicken colonel all ready to greet the general; his face fell as the door opened to two Red Cross gals in battle dress. We stayed for lunch and took off again to find the division. The pilots zeroed in on a group of farm buildings where the C.P. had been. We buzzed the place five times, banking over a ridge of hills. (About this time I had to make use of the *Stars and Stripes* I had in my lap, and not to read!) We dropped notes, but no response. So we flew on and landed at an airstrip where we hoped to be picked up.

Part of an armored group was stationed there, and all the guys came running out, ecstatic as we deplaned! They took us on a tour of what was left of this bombed-out airbase. I have official photos of the wrecked German jet planes on the ground there which were something brand new. The guys took some instruments off one and handed them to me:"Souvenir!" They showed us the big red parachutes, each panel made of two-inch heavily stitched bands with spaces between, two of which opened up behind to slow down these small jet-propelled planes for landing. One chap took out his pocket knife and cut out a couple of gores for another souvenir. And then we had a hair-raising ride around the field in a General Sherman tank. "See where the Jerry 88 went clear through—in one side and out the other. Three of our guys were killed in this one."

About four, we flew back and buzzed the farmhouse again but with no better luck, so it was back to the armored airstrip for the night. Chow line was in a bombed-out hangar, and we ate from mess kits in a circle around an open fire. Later they gave Stevie and me the only room they could still lock in a bombed out building. They brought in a couple of folding cots, army blankets, and a chamber bucket.

We awoke next morning to find snow on the ground, but thank heavens our radio message had gotten through and there was transportation. We took off and started picking up signs—"Charlie company," and so on all starting with C like the division code name, "Champion." We passed a lot of artillery and big guns that were still in operation.

Finally we came to the little town of Bleckede on the Elbe River and were told that the division C.P. was at the far edge of town. We arrived at the large two-storied white

frame house just in time for lunch with some top brass—
our general staff, General Matthew Ridgeway (head of all
U.S. airborne) and British Field Marshal Sir Bernard Montgomery (Monty) of the 21st Allied Army Group, who were
making plans to meet the Russians up ahead. We just sat
and listened.

They took off right after lunch, turning over this big
house to us and the two pilots and crew chief. Captain Patterson (a southern-gentleman type) was to see we always
had decent places to live. He assigned us two GI orderlies.
One came in sheepishly to ask what he had to do. He may
have thought we'd have him washing out panties or something. We told him just to sweep the place and keep the
fires going, especially in the big cookstove in the kitchen.
That would be our gathering spot.

This little town of Bleckede was where the 82d had
crossed the Elbe the night before under heavy fire. They'd
built a pontoon bridge (a line of flatboats with planks on
top) for vehicles and artillery. The men had crossed in funny little boats called "alligators" and "ducks."

Later articles in the 82d's own newspaper, the *All-American Paraglide*, said more about this crossing. Over a picture
of General Ridgeway and Field Marshal Montgomery standing beside a big army truck on the pontoon bridge, the
headline read: "82d Elbe Bridgehead Last in Europe. First
and Last European Bridgeheads Accredited to 82d Airborne
'Troopers.'" The first paragraph explained:

Bridgehead-Beachhead No. 11 for elements of the 82d "All American" Airborne Division was made on April 30 when the 82d
crossed the Northern Elbe at Bleckede for the last bridgehead of
the European War. It is befitting that the skyborne soldiers who
made the last bridghead assault were also in on the initial assault
at Festung Fortress Europa two years before when they made the
D-Day drop into Sicily July 9, 1943.

A slightly tongue-in-cheek article titled "Two Down and
One to Go: The Private Observations of a Private 82d Trooper" told what it was like for some of the guys.

On the evening of the 28th of April our lieutenant gave us the good news. We were to have the dubious honor of being the first to cross the Elbe River on a night patrol. Up till now we had felt fairly safe, the war was a long way off and all over but the fighting . . .

The next night the 82d led by the 505th Parachute Infantry, crossed the Elbe at the point we had patroled. In the days following, the 82d made long slashes into enemy territory, netting us a captured C.P., countless prisoners, and a complete disruption of enemy communications. . . . Then we drove through to the Russian Army only five miles from our main force.

For three hours we drove through a road clogged with men and materiel of a defeated army. . . . Tiger tanks with 88s broken and many growing rusty; flak wagons, their muzzles pointed skyward. But the German weapons still kept their sinister appearance, for we had seen them all before under much different circumstances. Heavily fortified positions were now harmless; ruined rifles and helmets littered the ground. The 21st Army had surrendered to the 82d Airborne Division. The crushed German Army . . . which lived by the sword has died by the sword. . . .

The Ruskies are a rugged looking lot of boys. Every one had a hat of curly black hair with a Red Star in front of it. Blouses with huge epaulets, baggy pants with black boots, just as you have seen them in pictures. It seemed every one had an automatic; most had long swords dangling to their toes. Although rather violent in nature they are cheerful and friendly. All Russian soldiers salute, then shake hands with you. Getting into the spirit of things the Yanks were all saluting as if we'd done it all our lives. . . .

This is the end of our war over here, so little else remains to be told. Everyone is busy figuring out their points or sweating out that P.F.C. (Pacific First Class!)

That first night we were in Bleckede the Jerries dropped strings of flares to light up the location of the bridge. We expected they'd try to bomb it, but they didn't. The Germans of Bleckede had been given twenty minutes to evacuate, so none were there when we arrived, but they started returning a day or so later. Our own GIs were playing "ugly American"; looting was the order of the day. About fifteen of them found new motorcycles. Everyone, it

seemed, had a bicycle, with or without tires. We got fresh
asparagus out of a garden and fresh rhubarb too, which I
hadn't tasted in ages.

When I went over to the mess hall—two doors down in
a brick house—to get sugar for the rhubarb, the mess sergeant said, "Hey, Vi, we've got a lot of beautiful canned
goods down in the basement. Come on down. Maybe
you'd like some of it." I still get kidding about the new approach: "He didn't ask you to come up to see his etchings,
just to come down to see his canned goods!"

It was fun doing our own cooking on a stove that reminded me of the big kitchen at Uncle Charlie's farm in
Minnesota. Of an evening, if the men who stopped by got
hungry, one would take his 45 and go out to "liberate a
chicken" for us.

Fellows found lots of stuff buried in gardens, including
cases of liquor, which made them dig further. I have a
whole supply of fancy scissors one GI brought over; he
said, "Vi, the mail room is in a hardware store. Anything
you need from there?" I heard there was a boot shop, a fur
store, a china shop, and more. I didn't get to see or explore
any of them, for one morning Captain Patterson dropped
by to tell us to be ready to move in half an hour. After
breaking our necks getting all packed up, we waited impa-
tiently—for four days!

They delayed our going forward after finding terrible
road mines. The Jerries had dug in from the side of a mac-
adam road and put boxes of explosive there with a kind of
cog arrangement set for a given number of vehicles. The
vibration of a vehicle would trip it a cog at a time. Possibly
nineteen cars could safely pass, and the twentieth would
be blown to bits. We lost I don't know how many jeeps,
trucks, and guys to those mines before they were cleaned
out.

We finally left with Captain Patterson in a command car,
headed for Ludwigslust, where 82d had met the Russians
and the whole German 21st Army (about 150,000 men) had
surrendered to General Gavin. The next four and a half

hours were some of the most poignant and unforgettable of my whole life. It took us those four and a half hours to make the thirty-mile trip, for after we crossed the pontoon bridge we'd move about fifty feet and have to stop. We were the only vehicle going east. Coming toward us were two and three lanes of traffic on a two-lane road—a parade of the most bizarre vehicles and forlorn human beings I've ever seen.

Fields on either side of the road were solid with human beings! German soldiers from generals down, looking as though each was their last step; men, women, youngsters and babes, feeble old folks—some together, others alone, all on foot, many bent under backbreaking loads of all those things they couldn't leave behind. On the road there were buses jammed to the roof and with fifteen or twenty people on the top, vans, trucks, civilian cars, motorcycles, wheelbarrows, bicycles, baby buggies, wheelchairs with those who couldn't walk. There were miles and miles of horse-drawn wagons, some with a rug or blanket draped over a long pole as a roof against the cold drizzly rain.

There was no frustration at being held up; we became part of that piece of history, that sea of humanity in a passing parade. It somehow didn't belong in the twentieth century—thousands and thousands of people, each a living moment of the dispossessing misery, pathos, and emptiness of war. GIs were frantically trying to keep the traffic moving; but the roadsides had been cut down into the muddy ditches, and vehicles would get stuck or run out of gas. To break such a jam our GIs would get German prisoners to push a stalled truck off the road or just tip it over—some exulting with language that wasn't pretty in their power over even German generals, who seemed to have no belligerence left in them.

The mood changed instantly as we entered Ludwigslust late that afternoon. The atmosphere was electric! People were everywhere—German prisoners, displaced persons of every nationality, the conquering Russians and Americans. Streets were lined with stacks of German helmets, piles of

rifles, and ammunition taken from the prisoners. Russian
tanks towered above the crowd, and hundreds or thousands of crazy Russians rushed about like children let out
of school. Now and then we saw a strange unmilitary uniform—actually a prison suit, the stripes nearly obliterated
by fifth and stains as it hung on a living skeleton who had
somehow found strength enough to walk the four miles
from the concentration camp 82d had liberated.

In this town of turmoil, which had been home to about
30,000 Germans, we looked for the division C.P. and finally
found it in the palace of Herzog von Mecklenburg-Schwer-
in, a multistoried gray stone building with an expansive
front entrance of columns and fancy copings, all duplicated
in the reflecting pool that stretched for several blocks down
the mall. Behind the palace were acres of beautiful gardens
and parks.

We reported in, and Captain Patterson took off to find us
a place to live after we said we'd rather not be billeted in
the palace. Meanwhile, we started touring the place. It was
like a museum with its high ceilings and ornate copings,
many walls diplaying lovely paintings. A wide, gracious
staircase led to the grand ballroom. Individual bedrooms
each had bath and sitting room. And the generals' offices!
General March had one of those little reverse-curve love
seats where you sort of formally face each other with your
feet on opposite sides. We tried it out, and some of the officers nearly died when I asked the general if he used it often. He's a bashful chap!

Finally Captain Patterson returned to drive us to our new
home, an apartment above a small tailor shop they had
taken over for us. He and a lieutenant brought over two
chickens, a couple of pounds of butter, bread, jam, and so
on. We fried the chickens and some potatoes and ate about
2:00 A.M.

The next day we had time to really see what had seemed
so exciting the evening before. The scene was stark by the
light of day, and we had a better chance to marvel at the
Russian soldiers. They were a grubby lot of all ages, some

awfully young, and even some women. We heard that they didn't have facilities like our mess halls but often had to live off the land as they moved along. Their uniforms looked it—baggy, mud-stained, coarse gray stuff they'd probably worn for months, ill-fitting trousers tucked into black boots. A GI told me he saw a woman officer discipline a Russian soldier by whipping him across the face with her Sam Brown belt. As I observed them there seemed to be what I can only think of as a dour denseness, which made us wonder what was going on in the minds under the red-starred caps.

Guess I should explain that all this time I was on temporary duty from the 17th Airborne Division and really should have reported back to France from Cologne. But I'd gotten so caught up in the excitement of going forward, that I'd put it out of my mind. Anyway, Colonel Ireland, our G-1 (in charge of personnel and administration), wanted me to stay and said he'd contact ARC headquarters, through 18th Corps; when they wanted me, the 82d would fly me back.

I kenw there was slight chance of its working that way; but it would be a good story to tell headquarters if I got into difficulties. This went on my list of the "lessons of living" I'd distilled from my experiences: if there's something you really want to do, and you're willing to take any consequences, then do it!

So, when Dottie (another of the Red Cross girls assigned to 82d) came up by plane, she said she had seen the ARC airborne supervisor in Paris a week before. When the super heard I was in Germany she said, "Heavens sake, isn't that girl back yet? Tell her to report to 17th division immediately." But neither plane was there just then, so I forget about it for more unforgettable days.

The concentration camp about four miles out of town had no ovens—it was just a prison camp. At first I didn't think I wanted to see it, and Captain Patterson (southern gentleman that he was) felt strongly it wasn't a thing American women should see. But one night at the C.P. when the

guys were damning all the "krauts" and saying, "We ought
to push them all in the ocean, or off the top of the
Zugspitz" (the tallest mountain), my German dander sur-
faced: "Maybe the German people didn't even know the
camps were there, or if they did, to speak out against them
may have meant their neck. For instance—what could you
do when you got your "invitation" from the president?
And remember you live in a democracy!" At that outburst,
Captain Patterson got so angry his face reddened, and
through clenched teeth he said, "You go out to the camp.
I'll see that you get there. Then you'll change your mind."

I did let some of the guys take me out. Truthfully, you
can see scads of pictures and be horrified but still not believe it when you see it with your own eyes. It all looked
OK outside, with about ten barrackslike brick buildings.
But inside! I can still see the double-deck cages faced with
chicken wire, and the green raw potatoes lying in the mat-
ted straw partially covering concrete floors. The reek of
personal filth in individual cages and the stench of the
dead were overwhelming. In fact, it was hard to tell the
living from the dead. Many looked like discarded, crum-
pled, fifthy striped uniforms dumped in a little pile on the
concrete floor of the cages. Now and then one uniform
would stretch out an emaciated arm, and two prisoners
managed to lift their caps to their liberators. But even those
living didn't seem human somehow with their skin a horrible greenish parchmentlike covering pulled tightly over
high cheekbones.

The powers that be had not bothered that day to remove
the dead; we actually stepped over bodies right in the
pathways between the cages. I wanted to stop breathing,
and almost to stop looking, as we passed one large room
where hundreds of bodies had been thrown in a huge pile
like so much trash. My senses revolted, and my stomach
too, at seeing bones and a part of a human body lying outside one building, as though dogs had left it there.

This was one of the days when they marched citizens of

surrounding villages through the camp to show them what their country had done. The men and boys were carrying shovels, and the women had sheets. As they waited outside the buildings, an American officer standing above them on the hood of a jeep explained why they were there. As they listened, most stood stolidly, staring without looking.

One of the GIs who'd brought us out had a case of Palmolive soap and some candy and cigarettes he wanted to take to a camp of Polish women they'd heard about. We found it nearby. As we drove in the gates of the barbed-wire enclosure, the women recognized something—our Red Cross bumper markings or my uniform—and made a dive for the truck. We didn't have to worry about how to distribute the little we had among six hundred women or more. They took things into their own hands, literally, fist fights and all. We just stood there and watched. It wasn't a pretty sight.

I talked with some of the men in charge and said I'd try to arrange to bring out some food. A GI who spoke Polish interpreted as we talked with the women. We learned that they had worked eight hours a day in a field and ten to twelve hours in a factory every day and evening, with rations of one loaf of black bread and a little grease each week. If they were caught making rosaries, or stole as much as a sugar beet or a piece of thread, their heads were shaved and they got nothing at all to eat for several days.

When we were ready to leave, we found the parade of German men and women who had toured the concentration camp passing by on the road. One of the GIs yelled, "Let's open the gates!" They did just that, and the guys stood there cheering as the Polish women, almost instinctively it seemed, streamed out and tackled German women, throwing some to the ground, taking their coats, shoes, stockings, and whatever they could. Even as the German women screamed, the German men stood stolidly by with blank stares. It was frightening to see humans so close to becoming animals. One could only wonder what it would be like to be one of the Germans, or to have gone through what the Polish women had endured.

But we had not yet witnessed all the horrors. Since none of our donut-making equipment had arrived yet, Dottie and I explored the town on foot. Toward the southern edge we were attracted to a huge gate behind which we found hundreds or perhaps thousands of people of all nationalities (Polish, French, Dutch, Austrian, and Italian we later found out) aimlessly milling about, wanting only a place to rest and food for their empty stomachs. The gate led into an old cavalry stable.

With the stupendous tasks facing it, the division had as yet made no provision for feeding these displaced persons (DPs), and we learned they'd already gone two days without food. As we watched, the thought of doing our Red Cross bit by serving coffee and donuts to our well-fed GIs seemed almost sacrilegious. I remembered that my supervisor had ordered my return to clear from 17th and perhaps be assigned somewhere else, but I felt needed here and once again willing to take the consequences. Stevie and Dottie and I decided to see about the possibility of setting up some kind of soup kitchen.

We went to the C.P. to talk with Colonel Marin, a G-4 (supply), officer, and he said what we expected to hear: "You gals are here to take care of our boys. Nobody will give you credit for feeding thousands of DPs. That's our job." But finally he told us he'd heard of a German warehouse in town. "I'll find out where, and if there's anything in it you can use, you can have it."

We went to the motor pool, and Dottie commandeered one truck to "try to scrounge some field ranges." I took a couple of two-and-a-half-ton trucks to look for the warehouse. And glory be! What we found did seem made to order for a soup kitchen, vegetarian style. There were stacks of dehydrated red cabbage, carrots, rutabagas, all in square blocks neatly wrapped in cellophane (about the size of old-fashioned honeycombs), and hundred-pound bags of dried peas, dehydrated potatoes, and flour. On straw in a corner was a mountain of black bread, green with mold and hard as rocks; we threw this on the trucks along with the rest. Finding some German SS insignia and papers on the floor as we left the warehouse made us realize that many who were now prisoners of war had undoubtedly hidden there, torn off their insignia, and discarded identification before facing their captors.

The cavalry stable buildings themselves, the DPs only shelter, were impossible, with filthy straw- and manure-covered floors, so we set up outside on the cobblestones. GIs brought tarps, and as we threw the moldy bread off the truck we had a minor revolution: the hungry mob rushed in, pushing, shoving, and fighting for a chance to grab a loaf. We fought them back and stationed a picked few as guards to prevent a riot. Even so, the front line kept moving forward inch by inch till sea of pale, blank, wild-eyed faces stretching across the compound became alarming.

Colonel Marin heard what we were up to and stopped by, aghast and concerned. "How are you gals going to control them—they'll mob you!" I made my way through to find a sergeant I knew who spoke several languages—at least Polish, German, and French. I put him on the hood of a jeep above the mob to explain to them why they had to wait and give us room. Whether they understood, no one could tell. Each stolidly stood his or her ground. The sergeant said, "No use, Vi. I can't budge them. Tell you what, I'll get Joe. He can speak any language in the book. Maybe they'll listen to him."

Joe came pushing through the crowd in his filthy striped uniform and little pillbox cap. Instantly, one sensed an indomitable spirit even the concentration camp had not been able to crush. There was a jaunty air about him, but his gaunt face became serious as he begged us, "Please do not judge these people as you see them here, Miss. Not long ago most of them were just as respectable as you. But after living in hunger, want, and fear for so long, they've become like the animals you see who must fight to live."

He jumped up on the jeep and spoke in several languages—in a kind, pleading way, and then with sharp commands—but with little result. As I watched I thought of the policing job it takes to keep happy, healthy Americans in line along parade routes at home and wondered why we thought we could move these desperate people with mere words. I thanked Joe and went back to the "kitchen."

As I approached, I had to smile, recognizing a feeling I'd experienced many times—that one of the biggest factors in our success in the war was the sense of humor of the American GIs. No matter how rough a situation, if one can find something to laugh about, the problem is lightened if not licked. They always could. Here was Louie, merrily whacking away at the bread with a meat cleaver, his brainstorm for solving the "dividing of the loaves." Bill met me with, "Which of the six delicious flavors do you want in this pot, Vi?" We decided on carrots and peas and put some of the people to work with hammers to break up the blocks of dehydrated vegetables and put them to soak in water in the huge GI cans that look like our big garbage cans.

Late in the afternoon we set the stuff cooking, and when the aroma of food finally hit the cold damp air, it brought the hungry crowd inching still farther forward so we could hardly work. But there seemed nothing we could do. Then a thought struck me that pushed everything else from my mind. I cried out, "Dottie, we've thousands of people and gallons of soup—what are we going to serve it in? We can't just have them hold out their hands." We stopped, stymied. What happened next still seems to me a modern miracle. As I tell it to you now, it truly seemed we had a silent partner in this operation. A captain had pushed through the crowd unnoticed; now we looked up as he called to us: "I'm with an engineering outfit fifty miles back. Came over to see the Russians and heard about this place. Decided to check it out. Just heard what you said, and would you believe it—we're stationed in a pottery factory!" For a moment we were speechless—but just a moment. By nine o'clock that night we had four six-bys, each loaded with new pottery bowls stacked high in excelsior!

What's more, those trucks solved the crowd dilemma too. Whose idea it was I'm not sure, but someone said, "Let's use the trucks." So the drivers lined them up four abreast and slowly backed the mob as though they were a herd of cattle. It seemed inhuman, but it did the job! Then, putting guards on the pushed-back mob, they backed two trucks together into a V and moved the others alongside as barricades. We were in business! The mob funneled into the V as the guards released them, and each received a bowl from a smiling GI sitting on a truck tailgate. Dottie and Stevie and I ladled thick steaming soup for hours. Behind us, Louise and another compadre gave each a large nugget of moldy black bread. They soaked the rock-hard bread and greedily drank from the bowls.

And again we had to put guards on the crowd so they couldn't slip back for seconds. I was panicky at the thought that we might not have soaked or processed the dehydrated stuff long enough, and what it might do in the shrunken stomachs of these sad souls. But I put that out of my mind, thinking we'd face that if it actually happened. Long after midnight our mission was accomplished—for that first day.

The next day brought organization. A local bakery was put into operation to bake fresh bread, which we served with soup at seven, twelve, and six. Between times the 325th Parachute Infantry Regiment sorted the people by nationality and moved them out to other camps. This didn't put us out of business, though; as each group left, others arrived, from where we didn't know.

Etched in my mind are those eager faces that first night. No, that's not the word; they lacked the human quality of eagerness. What we saw was more like an instinctively determined, driven force, reflected in wide eyes that seemed too large in their sunken sockets. Among the most pathetic were the political prisoners who had found strength enough to leave the concentration camp in their baggy, stained, striped uniforms. Most seemed walking death; one who couldn't stand any longer collapsed in the line. We moved him over to a pile of sand, and I set a bowl of soup beside him in a hollow scooped out of the sandpile. He couldn't even eat. I had to turn back, for the line was moving and needed me.

In the following days we had more time to talk with the DPs and see them as individuals. I found myself speaking German in a way I didn't realize I could; they actually seemed to understand. Many begged us to help them find their families, or wanted to know where they were and how long it would take them to get home. One man haughtily insisted that he was a Dutch ambassador and should receive special treatment. A frail, tiny old woman stopped the whole line one evening when she fell to her knees, took my hands in both of hers, and sobbed in German that she would never forget us and our wonderful food. I was crying too.

A little Dutch boy of about fourteen told me he had been taken from school and made to dig trenches. They had a work quota each day on a starvation diet. "I was strong and could endure; some of the older men could not." Then he continued in his halting English, "I have read your books. I love your detective stories. But now, the first opportunity I have to speak with an American, I cannot find the words." Others told us a small cup of our soup was worth ten bowls of what they had received from the Germans. Some Italians hungered for meat, which we could not provide. So when they spotted a stray horse, they took matters into their own hands, cooking the meat over small open fires. We eventually did arrange to get milk from the division for those whose digestions couldn't tolerate our soup, and for mothers with babies.

On Sunday we loaded bread and a huge GI can of soup in a weapons carrier (like a pickup truck) and headed for a camp of some four hundred Hungarian women on the edge of town. As we drove up, one woman of about fifty years old came running out to the truck. She couldn't speak English but took my arm to lead me to the building. The way she looked up at me gave me the oddest feeling— as though I were God. And perhaps to her it seemed that way. A mother and daughter spoke English; the twelve-year-old said, "Oh, we've heard all about you. One of the Hungarian boys from the camp was over today and told us the three wonderful American girls, and how beautiful you were." I still smile at that, for it had been raining, and we were filthy from moving the whole kitchen into a small corner of the stables we had cleaned out. But again, even though we were anything but glamourous in damp field coats stained with soup, they saw the real beauty of friendship, understanding, compassion, and love, in addition to the food.

It was hard to tear ourselves away. They wanted to talk, to tell of how they too had worked in fields during the day and in German factories at night on little food. Each day they had stood in fear as a German woman supervisor would stand in the door making a list of the weakest, who would later be taken away. "We never saw them again and always wondered." None of them knew where their families were, whether still alive or not.

We were criticized by some of the military who said we were being taken advantage of, since this was really their responsibility. But since our Red Cross equipment and supplies still hadn't caught up with us, it's an experience I wouldn't have missed for the world. I thought of the letters I get from some of you back in the States complaining about the rationing. Had any of you been able to share this with us, you would never again have complained. These thousands had no food at all—absolutely none—and worse still, nothing to go back to!

Every now and then I'd think, "But *you* do have to go back!" Then once again I purposely missed a C-47 flight so as to have an extra day to attend another unforgettable ceremony. I keep using that word, but truly, being a part of this unbelievable human drama will, I'm sure, so program my mind that I will never forget it.

This Tuesday morning was the mass funeral for the more than 250 victims of the concentration camp. We knew now why the villagers who were taken through the camp had had to bring shovels and sheets. Other German citizens had made white crosses to place at the head of the graves they were made to dig in long, long lines stretching out in the mall from the palace. In front of each grave was laid a body covered with a white sheet. Thousands strong, the citizens of Ludwigslust and surrounding villages were made to march past and view the bodies of those their country had persecuted. With them, too, came five Wehrmacht generals and other German officers—officers of an army that had sanctioned this giant crime against justice, decency, humanity. It was a sobering experience.

Next morning we were awakened by a GI who stopped by to say, "Colonel Norstad will pick you up any minute, Vi. He's flying back to Sissone." There was no putting it off any longer. I jumped out of bed and started dressing. He came just as I was brushing my teeth, and we whipped out to the Luftwaffe field and took off in his Norseman.

❧

Many years later I learned that April 25, 1945, is a more important date than most of us realize. It celebrates not only the meeting of the Americans and the Russians at the crossing of the Elbe but also the meeting of Allied statesmen in San Francisco for the founding of the United Nations.

An Elbe Alliance was founded based on the Oath at the Elbe, which has sponsored celebrations over the years. On April 25, 1985, at Torgau, Germany, their second Oath was taken: "We, Soviet and American war veterans assembled here today, forty years after the historic linking up of our allied troops on the Elbe River, once again reaffirm our allegiance to the pledge made by our comrades in arms on April 25, 1945, to dedicate our lives to furthering friendship between the peoples of the USSR and the USA so that wars never happen again."

10 V.E. Day and the Beginning of the Occupation

V.E. Day in France seemed almost anticlimatic; but it did bring the occupation with several troop movements involving difficult logistics and no time for letters home. So I continue from the small volume of journal notes I did send in June.

Sissone, France, Tuesday, June 12, 1945

Colonel Norstad let me fly copilot all the way down. It was exciting in that little plane. He'd point out things of interest, like how Hitler hadn't realized that when he built the autobahns he helped pilots navigate right to the important centers. He showed me how to read maps and then let me help navigate. As we flew over Cologne he circled the cathedral spires so I could see what precision bombing they had done to leave that beautiful edifice standing. The slender, peaked, lacy steeples reaching to the sky from the flattened areas all around were even more impressive from the air than on the ground. Over the Bulge area we saw devastation, the whole country pockmarked with bomb craters. By contrast, much of Germany seemed untouched, and it was interesting to observe camouflage of airports and military installations.

It was a long trip, and we stopped again at Braunschweig to refuel. We landed here at Sissone, which is base camp for the 82d, but I had to remember that I was still technically assigned to 17th Airborne. In the morning I called my supervisor in Paris, only to learn that she was in Germany and would be back on Friday. So I celebrated V.E. Day in Sissone. The French really whooped it up with a huge parade. We joined them in a noisy snake dance around the village square and later had our own private celebration, drinking champagne out of metal canteen cups.

On Friday after V.E. Day the supervisor called to tell me to report into Paris on Monday. I flew down and was soon waiting in the anteroom of Miss Hamer's office, wondering what I was in for. As I was seated across the desk from her, she smiled and said, "Well, how did you like 82d Airborne?" I told her I thought it was a neat outfit and that it had been an exciting experience, one I wouldn't want to have missed. Then she said, "I'm glad. Here's the idea. I'd like you to go back with them as senior club director. We need someone like you to take overall charge. You'll have the five regular gals under you."

After half expecting to be called on the carpet for not coming back, I could relax. Though I wondered how the girls already there would appreciate my coming in on top of them, who was I to turn down such an offer? She went on: "It will be your job to coordinate the regimental clubs for the division, decide which girl should be assigned to which club, find buildings and furnishings for clubs, supervise hiring of help and the central donut kitchen, coordinate supplies, make reports . . ." It sounded like a big job, but if she thought I could do it, I would.

We piled into her jeep and got back to Châlons about three to pick up what I'd left there. While she waited, I once again packed all my worldly belongings and said goodbye to friends. She took me to the airstrip to fly back here to Sissone. On the way I kept saying to myself, "The charm's still working!"

The next day we had word from 82d forward staff that there was a convoy moving down, and we could use the trucks to move all our operations forward to Ludwigslust. There was a big Red Cross club operating here in Sissone and one at Suippes, about sixty miles away. I made arrangements to turn all furniture back to the warehouse, dismissed the French help, and sent the two girls to Paris to clear their books. Then the trucks came in a day and a half ahead of time. So they flew me back to Suippes to pack the gals' belongings, which had to go on the convoy. We were all to leave by plane on Sunday, May 26. This time we *flew* into Ludwigslust! We were quartered in the same place, but with the addition of the sweetest Latvian maid, who did everything for us.

By then the donut operation had started, so I just stepped it up. Spent one whole day unloading the fifteen truckloads of supplies. What a mess! One truck had tipped over, and much of the stuff was spoiled. The rest had gone through rain, which didn't help things.

The regiments were greatly spread out, so we started a kind of clubmobile operation, serving a regiment a day. That was special for the guys, but it wasn't an easy job for us. Most evenings we'd be at the headquarters club in Ludwigslust. All of us had the privilege of riding beautiful beige Austrian mounts from the palace stables. The guys found a way to gamble and had a fancy setup of horse races on which they bet thousands. All this was written up in *New York Times*, which reported on their "Sauerkraut Downs."

About a week later we were commanded to provide the female touch at a big social function at the palace in honor of the Russians. It was held in the grand ballroom—just like those one sees in the movies, with gilt-framed mirrors and fireplaces and huge crystal chandeliers.

As the party started, glasses were filled and lifted high. First we toasted Stalin. The Russians countered with a toast to Roosevelt (this was just after we'd had word of Roosevelt's death, so I suppose they should have drunk to Truman, but that didn't seem to occur to anyone). Then they toasted the commanding generals, back and forth. They'd bring a refill each time, and though the glasses were small, we told General Gavin we couldn't continue to bottoms-up all that liquor. He said, "Just fake it. We can't insult the Russians."

Then the Russians presented medals to our three generals, the regimental colonels, and six GIs. And were they whoppers! I'd have given my eyeteeth for one as a souvenir. All of this had to be done with interpreters, of course, for none of the Russians spoke English, and so far as I know none of us spoke Russian.

We had a buffet dinner prepared by a French-German chef who came with the palace, and again I thought of movies I'd seen—tables with white linen cloths to the floor, covered with platters of venison steaks, chops, chicken, and more. I was dinner partner to the 82d's General March. We were seated with one of the Russian generals whose English consisted of "OK." He was entirely bald, so we kept calling him "Billiard Ball," and then we'd laugh, with him joining in.

The sixteen-piece dance band from the 325th Parachute Infantry Regiment was a smooth outfit, but eventually the Russians sent back to their lines for an accordionist and pianist who could play their kind of music. They demonstrated some of their dances and wanted to dance with us. I tried and had to give up. Only Dotty pulled it off.

Late in the evening, as everyone was pretty high, Colonel Tucker got up on a podium and regaled us all with high and low spots in 82d history. Emotions built! At one point a chap let out a yell and crashed his glass into the fireplace. That set off the whole crowd, and I remember dancing on cracked glass!

The next morning we were out in front of the command post serving donuts to a special group. I told Colonel Ireland I wanted to talk a little business. He's the G-1 (Personnel) officer with whom we coordinate things. Did I tell you that G-2 is Intelligence, G-3 Operations, and G-4 Supply? They're all on the General Staff. At any rate, Irish said he hadn't had any breakfast, so he took me by the hand and we went to the palace kitchen. The GIs there fixed fried eggs and toast and coffee as we talked.

Aside from business, Irish told me that he'd been over to the Russian lines till five the morning before, arranging the party, and that during the process the tumblers full of vodka had laid him out; that's why he missed the party.

And he wasn't the only casualty. When Colonel B., a tall West Pointer in command of the 325th, was talking with the Russians on the second floor of some building, one asked him, "How do you jump out of a plane?" The story goes that Colonel B. proceeded to show him by jumping out of a second-story window.

We kept accumulating stuff—souvenirs or loot, depending on how you look at it. The guys found a German train on a siding near town, one car filled with Nazi flags of all sizes. They brought us some, and said, "There's a whole car full of adding machines and another with light bulbs."

On the Sunday just two weeks after I'd come back to Ludwigslust, we heard the weird rumor that we were headed back to Sissone. We had thought we were going to southern Germany; Bavaria had been our dream. So Monday morning I went to see Colonel Ireland, only to find that he was already gone. They said to sit tight. That was about 11:20 A.M. At 12:25 Lieutenant Mason of G-1 came up and said, "Vi, can you get out to the Luftwaffe field to make a one o'clock plane? You'd better get down and find out what's cooking." So I dashed home and threw a few things in my bag; I thought I'd be coming back on the plane the next day.

It was terribly rough, and we went up to 14,000 feet to get above the weather. I'd just grabbed a blanket to try to sleep when the crew chief came back to ask if I'd like to pilot the plane. They had the C-47 set on automatic pilot, where some kind of gyro mechanism, I guess, operates the rudders and ailerons and stick to keep the plane level. All I had to do was turn a little button "up" or "down" to maintain altitude. It was scary and exciting up there in the nose flying into the clouds and not being able to see a thing. General March was a passenger, and when I went back, he looked up and said, "Marvelous job!"

Back in Sissone I was waiting for Colonel Ireland in the office of the chief of staff when General Gavin, the 82d's top general, came in and sat down. "I want four clubs

opened by the time the troops get back here," he said. I
told him we'd do that if they'd get our equipment and supplies down, thinking to myself, "Here we go again!"

I left the next morning for Paris to find out about getting
our furniture back. I always enjoyed driving through the
countryside and villages, even though jeeps aren't all that
comfortable. In Paris I finished my business about one and
was invited to make a foursome at golf by Art Alexander,
my *Yank* friend there. But I didn't have suitable shoes, so I
asked him to have dinner with me instead at The Pot, that
lovely French restaurant, La Potinnier, where the chefs perform absolute miracles with ten-in-one U.S. rations by just
adding one of those tremendous French sauces.

On the way back to Sissone, we came up through
Chateau-Thierry and Rheims, where I got off to arrange for
furniture. I spent the next morning arranging for a tent setup in two regimental areas at Camp Chicago near here, and
in the afternoon located a big old cassern building (barracks) in Laon for another regiment. Laon is a fascinating
old town built on a hill with fortifications all around and a
spired cathedral right at the top that you can see for miles.

I'd found out that supplies were coming on the first
train with the guys, so I made arrangements to get 10,000
donuts a day from a kitchen in Rheims to meet the troop
trains (had quite a time dealing through an interpreter).
Spent another day hauling furniture out again, and one
whole afternoon going from the prefectors to the major to
the town hall on a regular red-tape runaround to get clearance on a lovely modern building I found in Sissone. With
all the gals back, we opened our clubs as I'd promised
General Gavin, on D-Day anniversary.

I have a great snapshot of Marlene Dietrich standing in
front of the tall wooden doors of an old cassern building,
with her skirt pulled up showing her million-dollar gams,
pointing to the chalked message scrawled on the high
wooden door, OPENING TONITE—LOUISE'S JOINT. Marlene
dropped in on us every now and then, and everyone loved

her. She'd put on an old field jacket and visit with the men, even eating outdoors from a mess kit with them.

That was so in contrast to another glamourous blonde over here as a reporter, and attracted to the 82d Airborne, they say, because Jim Gavin is the youngest single general, and handsome. We were asked to put her up. So in addition to the once-over-lightly the French women did to our little house, we took time to dig out the corners and spark things up. From the fields I created a lovely bouquet of red poppies, blue cornflowers, white daisies, and wheat stalks. She stayed with us one night and is quoted as saying later (miffed at not being invited to stay at the general's staff quarters), "Those god-damned Red Cross girls may be noble, but I'm not. I'll not stay there another night."

We started serving 18,000 donuts a day without opening a kitchen of our own. I got the engineering guys busy building trays to fit into a truck, which seemed to solve the problem of getting dounuts from Rheims. Then, just as everything got into full swing, there was a division review one morning. All the guys were brought together in a sea of faces looking up at General Gavin who was standing on the hood of a jeep. He was announcing plans for the 82d to move about July 1, I can't tell you where yet.

On Sunday, Colonel Ireland came over to tell us that we would leave here by Saturday to move a couple of hundred miles to another temporary stop before the big one! So, less than two weeks after opening our clubs, we've closed them, loaded four carloads of stuff, and sent truckloads of furniture back to the warehouse. It would almost be comical if it weren't so much damned hard work. You want to say to someone, "Make up your mind!" I'll surely be glad when we can settle down somewhere.

I told General Gavin I don't intend to open operations at this next stop. I'm tired of it, and I'm going to wait till the 82d does intend to stay in one place. We have two command cars to travel in; I talked the powers that be out of sending us by convoy, so we'll have a couple of extra days here by ourselves. That's how I happen to have the time to write this volume. Tomorrow we're going into Rheims to go through a champagne cave, something I've meant to do ever since being around here. We'll also be able to see the cathedral without sandbags, and the Little Red School-house where the German surrender was signed.

Before we left Sissone, I went to my first "prop-blast." It was a kind of initiation, for when a trooper had made five jumps, he got his jump wings; but he wasn't *in* socially till he'd been "blasted." These were regimental affairs, and each regiment had its special "blast receptacle," often a huge silver loving cup or a vessel they'd found in some castle or other.

At the officers' club in Sissone, initiates were lined up on a platform some distance from the regimental commanding colonel. He stood behind a table facing the ceremonial cup which was filled with a secret formula of straight liquors, out of which initiates had to drink without taking a breath for a count of three. Each initiate was called by name and given a command: "Captain Smith, forward right roll!" He'd have to jump off the platform, do a somersault to the right, and with luck come up right in front of the com-manding colonel with a salute. If the emcee wanted to give a certain officer a hard time, he'd motion the crowd to yell, "Malfuntion," and the poor guy would have to do it all over again. Once the colonel returned the salute, the initi-ate's drinking started, with the whole crowd counting "thousand one, thousand two, thousand three." Then he could stop drinking. But most often the emcee would signal the "long count," and spectators would drag out the "thou-sands" at his direction. At any rate, after that part of the ceremony, most initiates were feeling little pain! All drinks were on the house prop-blast night; there was a wonderful dance band, and we all had a wild wonderful time.

Epinal, France, Friday, June 29, 1945

We arrived here two weeks ago after a wonderful day's trip via Verdun, Metz, and Nancy, and were put up in a lovely modern hotel with built-in furniture and great bathrooms with hot water an hour a day! We felt we had it made for this stop, but all that good feeling was shattered when I checked the supplies we moved by train from Sissone and found stuff missing. The whole thing leaves me with a thick file of statements from everyone involved in this move, which will go up as far as the Washington office of the Red Cross.

As senior club director of the 82d, my report was six pages long, telling how supplies were loaded on a train at St. Erme near Sissone. A headquarters lieutenant had been in charge, and a private on our detail went with the shipment, sleeping in one of the train's four cars. Loading and unloading on both ends was done by the Triple Six Quartermaster Trucking Company attached to the 82d. At Epinal I found supplies haphazardly unloaded in a long building without locks and even missing one door. I was aghast when on June 19, I took inventory and found the following missing: 925 pounds of fat (twenty-five 37-pound cans); 500 pounds of coffee (twenty-five 20-pound cans); and 780 pounds of sugar (thirteen 60-pound bags). Of course, I immediately reported all this to Colonel Ireland.

A telling paragraph in Private Cogan's statement (just one of many from everyone involved) said, "At Epinal the trucks didn't go from the station in convoy to the warehouse. They went separately. So I couldn't have a guard on each truck. I went on with the last truck after inspecting the train to see that all supplies had been unloaded, and picked up several tins of coffee and one tin of fat which had fallen off trucks that had gone on ahead."

Somehow, between the train and the warehouse, one truck took off somewhere else for unloading. All these supplies were like pure gold on the black market. Maybe this gives you an idea of the headaches and responsibility that go along with this job. After all the Army paperwork involved with the investigation, I hope I don't end up paying for all that stuff!

As I said, I intended not to open clubs here, but the first

day a couple of regimental COs just happened into Irish's office and made a good case as to why the guys really needed something. So in forty-eight hours we had one beautiful division club opened in a cafe connected with our hotel. It's huge, with lovely booth arrangements and a big balcony with a bandstand, PA system and all. Besides that we have three regimental clubs and are opening another on Monday.

We were to have been here only ten days and I was to have left Monday with an advance party of ten by plane for Berlin, but plans have changed once again, and we'll be here a while. So, since it will be more difficult once we get up to that tight little island in the Russian zone, I'm sending the other girls on leave to the Riviera next Wednesday, and Glenna and I leave the following Sunday. When I went to tell Irish, he offered to send us down in the next plane.

"Oh no!" I told him. "We don't want to go to the Riviera!"

"Well, where do you want to go?"

"How about a vehicle and a driver and letting us take off?"

He said he'd see what he could do. Hope it works out. It's the first leave I'll have taken and I really need it, though the travels we have in mind won't be exactly a rest! At any rate Irish was wonderful about it all. In fact I get anything I ask for from him lately.

Before the gals left we had a wedding! Stevie was to have been married to her 505 major in Rheims. In fact, they had already printed invitations and made arrangements when we pulled out too suddenly. So we had it here in a lovely little church. And we arranged a dance for the guys at a large ballroom. Getting hostesses was a different matter than in England, for many French mothers don't trust the American GIs and insist on chaperoning their daughters. So we got more formal, with printed invitations:

LaCrois-Rouge Americaine 82d Division Airborne vous invite a une Soirée dansante qui aura lieu en la Sallel du Palais de la Biere a Epinal, le Samedi 23 Juin 1945 de 20 heures a minuit.

—la Croix-Rouge Americaine

Refreshments were little sandwiches and cookies and ice cream, and many moms were seen sneaking stuff—even ice cream!—into their big handbags.

There was another prop-blast, too, with dancing on an outdoor terrace alongside a beautiful lake and a full moon sending ribbons of sparkle across the water. This was a wilder blast than the one in Sissone, because many were bidding buddies goodbye. We had had word that high-point men were to be transferred to 17th Airborne Division, which was going home.

There have been lots of wild farewell parties at the hotel as well. One night we heard screams, and looking out of the window across the air well we saw a French gal being swung by her heels out of a fourth-story window! There were drunken song fests too, with "Berlin, Berlin, my heart is bleeding."

Talk of transfers reminds me—I had a call from Ellie, a Red Cross girl who's now with 17th Airborne. Some of her special guys who are low-pointers will be transferred to us, so she asked whether I'd try to get her transferred too. But I know that our girls don't particularly like Ellie, so I called Paris headquarters asking that she not be sent to us!

I was out at the 504th Parachute Infantry regimental area when Colonel Tucker was saying goodbye to a lot of his guys. It's one of the oldest paratroop regiments; men have been together through operations in Africa, Sicily, Anzio, and the bulge, and they'd do anything for Tucker. He had tears in his eyes toward the last, even though he's a tough baby.

When I checked back with Irish about our leave, this great guy handed me orders signed by General March, putting Glenna and me on TDY, temporary duty, to the 101st Airborne Division in Berchtesgaden; this way we can get entry into Germany, which still requires military orders. And we are to have a command car with a GI driver!

11 To Berchtesgaden and Back

Irish was there to see us off. As we were thanking him again for the imaginative orders to get us into Germany, we noticed the gas tank was leaking a few drops. I pointed this out. His blue eyes twinkled as he grinned and said, "Oh, just put some chewing gum on it!"

So we took off with Don, our GI driver, through lovely mountainous country to the fortress city of Strasbourg on the banks of the Rhine at the French border. When we stopped there just after noon to stretch out legs and nibble some K rations, a French chap came up, pointing to our gas tank, and our hearts sank. Gasoline was running out in steady streams.

We knew we had to do something. With French help we found a small American engineering outfit attached to the French army there. They put some German prisoners to work taking off the tank to solder it. The Americans entertained us royally all afternoon; we were the first American girls they'd seen in months, and they begged us to stay over that night. "We can get billets and we'll show you our night clubs and go swimming in the Rhine . . ." But we took off about five in the evening, crossing the Rhine into Germany.

We hadn't gone very far when we wondered whether we were in the right country. We saw black soldiers in GI fatigues (coveralls) but with a wide red sash beneath their pistol belts, and most were wearing brightly colored turbans. As we passed, one group let out with what we figured must be some kind of wolf call. Don nearly went off the road laughing. Eventually, we learned that they were Moroccan "wolves" who were in charge in this French-occupied territory.

The mountains of the Black Forest were exciting. We loved

Violet Kochendoerfer

From top: Violet Kochendoerfer
building a fire in the office at the
315th Troop Carrier American Red
Cross Club; entrance to the 315th
Club; General Jim Gavin of the 82d
Airborne Division

General Gavin speaking to the All-Americans of the 82d; *below,* survivors leaving a concentration camp liberated by troops of the 82d Airborne Division (U.S. Army photograph)

Above, 82d Command Post in Ludwigslust, Germany, where final surrender papers were signed (U.S. Army photograph). *Below,* 82d Airborne Division Troopers in front of the Command Post in Ludwigslust.

Vi with Hal and Clint, who supervised GI help at the 17th Airborne Club, Chalons-sur-Marne, France

Marlene Dietrich at the 82d club opening at Rambervillers, France, June 1945

Above, ARC Olympic Club, Garmisch, Germany, January 1946. *Below,* getting supplies for the Olympic Club in Garmisch. Vi is in the center. (Photo by Ollie Atkins)

Playing cards at the Olympic Club. *Below,* What To Do in Garmisch

Above, GI's at the Olympic Club. *Below,* Vi with Jimmie Worback and his dog Blackie, mascots of the 82d Airborne Division. Jimmie was born in Brooklyn and went to Sicily in 1939 with his German-born mother. After his mother was killed, he wandered over Europe as a GI mascot.

the picturesque chalets. But then a car passed us, its passengers pointing back and yelling "*Esssence, essence!*" That's "gasoline" in French. We stopped. Anger toward Irish welled up as I saw the gas tank leaking as badly as before the solder job. Though it was still light, it was after eight, and when shortly after moving on we were detoured over a little dirt mountain road, we decided to stop at the first village. That was Villigen. We pulled up where we saw a big French flag. This turned out to be a camp of Polish DPs, but one of the officers escorted us into the military government headquarters on the village square, where we were given credentials for a hotel room.

I had Don drain the tank so we wouldn't lose more precious gas. The military governor suggested we leave our extra gas in their office. Don brought in five jerry cans of five gallons each; closely eyed by the French. We couldn't help wondering whether it would be safe even there; like our missing supplies, it would be gold on the black market.

That evening at the hotel we talked about Irish again and then decided to take seriously what he'd said in jest. Luckily we had some gum, so next morning Glenna and I sat on the cobblestones beside the command car, chewing away. When all the sweetness was gone, we'd hand the stuff to Don, who was under the car smearing gum along the exposed seams of the gas tank. As we were right in the village square, a crowd gathered, and though they didn't say a word, I'm sure they were thinking "crazy Americans."

That morning the gum did seem to hold, and my feeling toward Irish mellowed a bit. We'd decided to put in one can of gas at a time, with the rationale that it wouldn't leak out as fast that way. That afternoon on the Arlberg Pass the road narrowed to a one-way affair. Just as we slowed for a sharp bend, we killed the engine and stopped. Then a jeep full of Frenchmen came along. Were we ever glad to see them and to learn that we were just fifty kilometers from American-occupied territory. They told us how to find the 103d Division, and our last can of gas took us to its rear command post at the edge of Innsbruck.

The sergeant in charge intimated we could stay there and introduced us to their interpreter, Adolph Huber (an instructor in Hannes Schneider's famous ski school), who was wearing the typical Tyrolean lederhosen—chamois shorts with wide felt suspenders. We talked skiing, and he told us what to see in Innsbruck. Then the sarge brought over an Austrian countess who was a nurse with their Red Cross. She spoke only German; but I got on well with Adolph's help in translating. I found that Austrian Red Cross women are all nurses. We traded pins—"talismans" she called them.

Innsbruck is a large city and popular resort town in a spectacular setting, with high mountains rising in its back yard. We left Don to get the command car fixed and serviced. At Adolph's suggestion Glenna and I took a cable car about six hundred feet up the mountain, where we had lunch at the 103d's forward command post. The cable car was a new experience for us. It was a glass-enclosed cubicle about eight feet long and four or five wide, suspended from a heavy cable. As motors pull one car up, the other comes down, swinging between huge pylons that hold the cables sometimes five hundred feet or more above the ground—scary!

A little over halfway up a big hotel with Tyrolean decorated rooms served as the 103d enlisted men's club. A Tyrolean band was playing, and the view of the valley below was breathtaking. Wearing my paratrooper jump boots, I danced a waltz with a GI. Then we took the last cable car almost to the top and found ourselves in a blizzard. We had to climb that last two hundred feet in snow over our knees—on the third of July!

We got back to find that the 103d's mechanics had taken gas tanks off six different vehicles before they found one that would fit ours. We left about five o'clock without waiting for chow, but at a later check point in the 42d (Rainbow) Division area, the MP insisted they could improve on the K rations we were eating. It was late, but they fixed fried eggs, toast, and jam.

We made Berchtesgaden that night and were billeted at the fabulous Berchtesgadener Hof, a sumptuous ultramodern hotel that Hitler built for his officers. The rooms opened onto wide balconies overlooking a fifty-foot plaza filled with tables and bright striped umbrellas, which in turn overlooked a classic picture of snow-capped peaks and all that goes with mountain scenery. The furniture was all white: glass-topped tables, and brocade-upholstered chairs—most unmasculine!—and beds with real "linen" linen and (instead of a blanket) a quilted edelweiss embroidered featherbed one hardly felt. The meals were superb too. I'd always thought of German cooking as undistinguished, but what the Germans there did with K rations was almost equal to the skill of the French.

Glenna had been with 101st at one time, so in the morning we went to the division C.P. to see some of her friends. One of them took us to see Field Marshall Wilhelm Keitel's command post. We knew he had been chief of staff of the German army, but we hadn't expected to see such a high-tech layout, with banks and banks of buttons and switches, in the Bavarian Alps.

That afternoon we went to see Hitler's *berghof* a short way up the mountain. It lay pretty much in ruins, but the bombing hadn't touched the shelter, built deep into the mountain, where what seemed kilometers of corridors led to several fully-furnished apartments, medical and dental labs, an operating room, barracks for guards, Eva Braun's apartment, and a room with blanks of switchboards for the telephone system. After seeing homes belonging to Martin Bormann and Hermann Goering (we loved Goering's giant bathtub!), we drove to Koenigsee, said to be the most beautiful lake in Austria. It stretches five long miles between snowcapped mountains that come steeply down to the water on both sides. We took a motorboat ride to one flat spot along the shore that formed a platform for a little onion-topped church.

That night I had a date with a major for the Fourth of July celebration at the lake. An elegant champagne and steak dinner at the Schiffmeister Hotel, with floor shows, dancing, and yodeling all seemed appropriate in that setting. Later, the make-do flares that came down on little parachutes and rocket guns reverberating between the mountains seemed so war like that we almost expected to see a band of SS troops come out to surrender. It was the most unusual unique Fourth I've ever spent.

There were trips to Salzburg and Wolfgangsee, and we drove up to Hitler's Eagle's Nest. The road to the 7,000-foot peak was a marvel, with the rocks of the roadcut alongside painted in camouflage colors. For the last two hundred feet we took an elevator from behind a big bronze vault door in the side of the mountain. The elevator was ten feet square with upholstered seats all around and a freight elevator beneath. The fellow that built it for Hitler was still its operator. We wondered just what he thought of us crazy Americans.

The hideaway itself was a lovely apartment with servants' quarters. A long, long table almost the length of one room was surrounded by carved high-back chairs. A big round table stood in the center of another huge room with window walls. The view there is inspiring—almost unreal—as one looks down over mountain peaks of five different countries. One could see how Hitler might dream that he was ruler of the world as he stood there. Yet we were told that Adolph had actually been to the Eaglesnest only five times, and at no time longer than two hours.

We thought we'd like to go home via Italy. We were told, "You can't get over the border without orders from a Fifth Army Group in the MTO, the Mediterranean Theater of Operations. What's more, there's bad typhus epidemic and they aren't letting anyone in." We still decided to try—especially after a colonel we met at a dance said, "I can fix your orders. Just look me up in the morning."

We did, and he helped us make a new copy of our orders, predating them to show that we had been on TDY with 101st Airborne for three weeks and adding, "at the completion of which they will report to the Riviera Rest Area for a seven-day leave." The rationale was that the powers at the border would let us go over the Brenner Pass instead of through Switzerland. As I typed in "By Order of Commanding General March," I felt a bit guilty. Glenna did the actual forging of the signature, and we took off.

Everyone had told us to be sure not to miss Grossglockner (which means big bell), the highest mountain peak and largest glacier in Austria. Mountain lover that I am, I talked us into going a hundred kilometers off course to see it. At the top we met Americans from the 10th Mountain Division who were there for a ski meet. When they found we were headed for the Brenner Pass, they said, "Why go all that way? You could leave here at one and in about eight hours be across the border into Italy and to our headquarters and rest hotel in Udine." So we decided against the Brenner and instead crossed the border in isolated British territory. We held our breath as we showed our orders. The guards looked at them and asked, "What outfit are you with?" "82d Airborne." They checked this marking on our command car bumpers and waved us through!

The atmosphere changed immediately once we were in Italy. Villas and stone fences and different church architecture caught our eyes. We followed directions to the 10th Mountain Division rest hotel, where dinner was still being served on a patio with soft lighting under a ceiling of live green ivy. It was a delightful atmosphere.

We left Udine early in the morning and arrived at Venice about noon. It didn't seem real to be there. We parked our command car in a big three-story garage, and the British bloke in charge told us how to get to St. Mark's Square. "You take a gondola from right down here. You'll need lira." When we explained that we didn't have any because when we left we never dreamed of being in Italy, he lent us five hundred, which was over $5.00 worth. I think Don gave him something to make it right. We went down to a dock, picked a fancy gondola with black-tasseled upholstery, and leaned back against the pillows, smiling in disbelief.

There was a lot of traffic on the Grand Canal. We were entranced at the way they guide the gondolas around, with funny noises to signal their coming around blind corners from little narrow canals all along the way. After seeing St. Mark's Square and the cathedral with people feeding pigeons as one sees in pictures, we got another gondola to go under the

Bridge of Sighs and Rialto Bridge. It was hard to tear ourselves away, but we left about five, picking up our car and heading toward Verona, where we thought we might look up the Red Cross girls. Surely there would be a club there.

Those thoughts were eclipsed by more car trouble—this time it seemed to be fan belt. A couple of GIs along the road took me to a headquarters building to call the motor pool, and once again we were taken care of. The guys there also suggested a great rest hotel on Lake Garda. We decided against trying to find the Red Cross in Verona after all, thinking that through them word might get out that we were illegally in Italy. We stopped a bit just at dusk to see the old castle of Romeo and Juliet and the Arena, and then drove on to the Fifth Army rest hotel on Lake Garda.

Its setting was spectacular, high above the lake, which at early evening was shimmering with lights. As we drove up, the captain in charge said, "Sorry, but we can't accept anyone without orders from the Fifth Army Group." As our faces fell, he grinned and added, "But we never turn anyone away." We had our first canned beer in years!

We were already two days overdue on our leave, but there was Lake Como, so often the setting for novels and movies. I had the feeling I'd never have another chance to see it, so though it was somewhat off the shortest route home, we checked the cross-country highways and took off. Once again I was using that little philosophy about taking the consequences.

Lake Como is like a big inverted Y, with Bellagio between the two legs. Don parked the command car at a downtown spot on the lake, and we all agreed to meet back there at three. I was entranced with the many narrow streets leading up the hill, which weren't really streets at all but steps with buildings on both sides. Intriguing shops made me want to buy something, but I had no lira. So I tried cigarettes as legal tender for the first time. We got about a dollar a pack for them. One woman in a linen ship wanted sugar, and I was able to buy some things with the little packages I'd saved from K rations.

Two American majors recognized me as American Red Cross and hoped we were staying over; they'd wine and dine us and we'd have a great time. I told them, reluctantly, we had to push on. We figured we had at least two days of hard driving to get back to Epinal. Our resolve didn't hold. We weren't three kilometers out of town before we'd talked each other into turning around, staying over, and getting up really early in the morning, rationalizing that we'd make just as good time. So back we went to the Albergo Splendide, an Air Corps rest hotel. When we told the captain in charge that we didn't have a lira between us but would like to stay, he not only gave Glenna and me the best corner room but provided some lira so we could swim at the lido.

As we headed up a wide staircase from the lobby, the two majors I'd met were coming down in swim trunks. They waited for us, and we boated up the lake for drinks and swimming. Once again, I just couldn't believe I was there! After dinner and an evening of dancing we wouldn't let them talk us into staying over again but stuck to our plan and left very early the next morning.

So much for plans: about twenty kilometers out on the road to Milan, the engine sounded as though it were surely malfunctioning. Don checked and reported that we didn't have any oil. I was furious! This trip was "duty" for him; he had only to see that the car was serviced and drive us where we wanted to go, and we'd included him in all our adventures. I felt he'd taken advantage of our good will and I wouldn't let him drive on. "You take off and find some oil. I don't know where, but don't you dare come back without it." He thumbed a ride and was gone.

About ten minutes later an army truck came along with a couple of captains from the hotel where we'd stayed. Upon learning of our predicament, they said, "You'd better let us push you into Milan." So one captain got behind the wheel, and the other in the truck started pushing us, one time even passing a car! They rolled us into the headquarters of the 4th Army Corps and called the motor pool to bring out some oil. The sergeant poured it in, listened to the engine, and said it sounded OK. But now where was Don? We'd forgotten all about him. All we could do was drive back to look for him. This time I got behind the wheel, even though command cars aren't the easiest things to drive.

Again about twenty kilometers out, there was a funny noise under the hood, and I decided we'd better go back. As I made the turn, there was a loud thud and a frightening clanking sound that said, "Stop!" and so for the second time that morning we were pushed into Milan—this time by an Italian truck. This time we were told that a connecting rod had "gone out," so they called ordnance. While we were at lunch, I looked up to see Don walking in to the very place we were waiting! How lucky could we be!

The wrecker came at three, but our troubles weren't over. As we backed our command car into position, the connecting rod flipped over and knocked a hole in the bottom of the oil pan. I was just about sick by then, but the fellows said, "Don't worry. That way it's easier to get a whole new engine." So we crawled in as they hoisted up the front end and got a sightseeing tour of Milan and its famous cathedral, swinging from the back of an army wrecker. Milan was a more modern city than I'd imagined. The girls were most attractive and well dressed.

The sergeant at the motor pool made out a slip: "Install new engine." I said, "That's awfully generous of you, but how long will it take?" When he said, "Oh, about two days," I was relieved. We got rooms at the 4th Corps Hotel.

Next morning I sent a radio message to Colonel Ireland, telling him that we'd be late getting back because of engine trouble. Then I got some of the general's surplus transportation to take us back to the lake while Don waited in Milan with our command car. Before we left, our driver took us to see Leonardo Da Vinci's famous *Last Supper* painted on the wall of the little refectory in a monastery that had been bombed. It was terribly faded and peeling but truly something to see.

This stay at the lake included swimming and an evening of dancing with handsome British South Africans, who sang us songs of the Transvaal as we rowed back from the lido. We loved their brogue and their slang. They'd say "bloody this" and "bloody that" and then beg our pardon; for to the British, "bloody" is a cuss word. They wore shorts and knee socks, and the uniform included a tam with a round tassel. I liked them a lot and surely had my mind changed about South Africa, which they said was very modern and patterned after the States. Then I was impressed; today, with their country constantly in the news, one can but wonder.

Don showed up next afternoon with a new engine in our command car. We left early in the morning, skipping Milan this time to cut across country through funny little towns where invariably the road narrowed to a little cobblestone street just wide enough for us to get through the people, carts, and bicycles. We'd wonder whether we were still on the highway! We drove through exciting mountain country. Many of the slopes were anciently terraced, and there were vineyards for miles, with now and then a castle. About five-thirty we drove into the tiny village of Coeur Maier, nestled at the foot of snowcapped Mont Blanc—the highest peak in the Alps. The OSS (Office of Strategic Services) captain gave up his room to Glenna and me and found something for Don. And after dinner at the home of friends he got in touch with the Frenchman who ran the cable car up the mountain, and we were privileged passengers for that command trip.

We slept that night with a rushing mountain stream just outside our window and left early the next morning after a bountiful breakfast. The jolly South African chap manning the border checkpoint at the top of Petit St. Bernard Pass just stamped our orders and waved us through. We were back in our own ETO, driving down miles of switchbacks with panoramic views.

The whole trip had not been just a B & B, but B & BLD—bed and breakfast, lunch and dinner. Our hosts that evening were the men of a U.S. engineering company who put us up in a huge estate, with German prisoners waiting on us in a private dining room. We got off at seven the next morning, and by driving till nearly midnight we arrived in Epinal just two weeks and four days after we had started. We had traveled something over 2,500 miles, and of course we sat up till all hours telling the other girls about the trip. They'd really worried about us and apparently missed us too.

In the morning we turned in the command car and reported to Irish. I told him I thought we should bill him for one totally reconditioned and almost internally replaced command car. He just listened and smiled—and didn't read us the riot act for coming back four days late.

12 The Berlin Story

When Glenna and I returned from our leave, there wasn't time to relax, just enough to give instructions to the four regimental club directors about how to get ready for the next imminent move, since I might not be there. I was to fly to Berlin with the advance party to find buildings and make plans for new ARC clubs.

With the 82d Airborne, I'd begun to feel more a part of the military than I did of the Red Cross. Paris was far away, and my supervisor seemed to feel I could handle things. General Jim Gavin was my new boss, and Colonel Ireland the supervisor I went to with requests and problems. Even though we moved so often it was hard for ARC headquarters to keep track of us, I credit this feeling to the 82d. We were considered a valuable part of that proud division. That pride permeated the division from general down to private. Top brass had the love and loyalty of all the men. I felt that General Gavin put a premium on what we contributed to that well-being and esprit de corps. At any rate, I was treated as an equal and could do things my way and with cooperation.

We were in Berlin for V.J. Day on August 14, 1945, as but part of a larger show, with the military of four nations involved. Americans, British, and French each had their own zone and saw less of one another than we saw of the Russians. After the victor-buddy relations we'd had with the Russians in Ludwigslust, it seemed ironic that we should feel almost captive on the little island of Berlin in the huge Russian zone, but that's the way it was.

I'd exclaimed as the advance party flew into Berlin, "I thought it was badly bombed!" Then I looked again and realized that what I had taken for OK apartment buildings and houses were often just shells; later, I saw plenty of rubble. When we landed at Templehof Airdrome, I found that only six jeeps had been flown up for the whole division. They did let me take one for a morning and a lieutenant and I checked out the Titania Palast, a big theater building which provided entertainment in Berlin for everyone, not just the 82d.

I had to give up the jeep at noon, but Colonel Ireland was trying to find a building for the division command post, so I joined him that afternoon driving around looking for possible C.P. and possible Red Cross club buildings. It turned out to be a good sightseeing trip through flattened sections between areas that weren't even touched. I was impressed that bombed areas were getting cleaned up, unlike many bombed French cities. The Germans bricked up blown-out windows to make a solid wall and then, by means of bucket brigades in which women took part, dumped the debris behind the walls.

Since I hadn't brought my personal stuff and really needed wheels that the division couldn't spare, I persuaded Irish to let me fly back to Epinal with him and drive our car up. We had dinner with General Gavin. When I mentioned I'd heard a rumor that we ARC gals might be taken from 82d, the general said, "If they try to move you, Vi, you just tell them they have to come to me. You've all been assigned to us and they can't take you away." Then he signed orders for me and two GIs to drive back to Berlin in our Chrysler convertible.

Yes, Chrysler convertible. After hostilities ceased, both officers and GIs had been driving around in automobiles they'd come by in many odd ways. When it got to be an open scandal, a directive came down that only field-grade officers (that would be majors and above) could have them; others had to turn their cars in. Their misfortune was our good luck: Colonel Weinicke, division chief of staff, told me, "Vi, Captain Miller just turned in a good Chrysler convertible. If you can register it with Red Cross, you gals can have it." So the car was registered in my name in Paris and then sent to Brussels to be painted olive drab with an official-looking military designation on the hood in big white letters and numbers. With its red leather upholstery and a rumble seat, the Chrysler was such a contrast with an army jeep that it became the talk of the division. We could ask almost anything in exchange for a ride in it.

I left the girls instructions for closing their clubs when their orders came and set out to follow my own orders: proceed, with two GIs, "on or about 30 July 1945 to Wiesbaden, Germany, and Berlin, Germany, in connection with Airborne Activities." Our first stop was historic old Heidelberg, where we spent the night. After our clubs in tents and makeshift buildings, we were impressed with the almost palatial Red Cross Club alongside a lake, with available boats, an opera house, lovely lounges, and, far up the hill, a huge modern swimming pool, tennis courts, and mineral baths, which we tried. I inquired, and was told that American WACS sometimes came to the club, but I didn't see one.

We went on to Frankfurt, which we found leveled in many areas. And from there we traveled on the *Reichsautobahn*, where Germany seemed to be way ahead of us. Each double lane was over twenty feet wide; with a median between, they looked like two wide white ribbons unrolling across the landscape. We didn't bother about speed limits, and there was a great feeling of freedom, just passing vehicles without worry about oncoming traffic. We were warned to watch for road blocks and signs switching us at times to the opposite side where a bridge on our side had been blown.

We expected to make Berlin the next day, but in stopping at Kassel for lunch we were told that to go through British or Russian territory we'd need special stamps on our orders from some office located an hour and a half back. We decided to spend the night in Kassel. We stayed at a British transient hotel where I was something of an oddity. A British sergeant in charge said he could provide dinner but didn't know about a room. I went to wash my hands and returned, expecting to join my GI companions. But the sarge had a table set up in a private room, where I had to eat all by myself (it was pretty much a "free-for-all in the dining room" as he put it), and he managed to find me private accommodations for the night as well.

Though I didn't go back for the clearance, we had no trouble driving through the Russian zone. In fact, it was something the three of us will never forget. Russian guards stood at intervals all along that two hundred miles on the autobahn. Because our car was the right color, with big official looking numbers on each side of the hood, they figured the GIs were officers and saluted us all the way into Berlin. Don and Phil loved returning the salutes. That situation would change drastically two years later, when that strip of road, known as the Helmstead Highway, was one that the Russians blocked off, forcing the organization of the Berlin airlift.

In the summer of 1945, however, we entered Berlin without trouble, leaving the autobahn at the exit for the Berlin Ring, which girds the city. We arrived in time for lunch with Colonel Ireland in the new mess hall they'd set up and then spent the afternoon reporting in, getting cleaned up, and picking up maps and directions so I could find my way around the city. I was to look for suitable buildings for an enlisted men's club in each of four areas marked on the maps, and another for the headquarters officers' club. The maps were so huge that I'd get all tangled up in them, and comparing them with the posted street signs wasn't easy. Before we discovered that the main drag changed names several times, we'd often be lost before we started. There were Russian signs too, with those funny upside-down letters.

With the maps, the captain in charge handed me a 32 automatic. I drew back, looking quizzically at it: "I don't like guns and I'll never shoot one." The way I held it scared the guys in the office and they sidled out of range! "Well, just keep it in the glove compartment and pull it out if you need to." I hoped that would never happen.

After I found a place for us Red Cross gals to live, I wrote home for the first time in weeks.

Berlin, August 8, 1945

These past days have been hectic again, but something new and different. Little Vi (there are two of us, so she got this title) had arrived from Epinal, so I have welcome company. I was looking for a house large enough for all of us and decided it should be somewhere around division C.P.

Imagine house-hunting for a furnished place that isn't too badly damaged, has a roof on and not too many windows out. We'd drive around and, when we saw a possible one, would knock, go in, and have the residents show us around. We had no special identification but were wearing American Red Cross uniforms and patches. Most Germans were polite, but behind that facade one just knew they hoped against hope that we wouldn't requisition *their* home. Some would point out problems, saying, "*Alles kaput.*"

We found one great place—three apartments in a beautiful sunken garden area, one furnished in true Hollywood style—and we decided "This is it!" Then we discovered that it was in the Group Control area, which is set aside for VIPs, very important persons. Everyone told us we wouldn't have a chance, but we could try. We tried; but it didn't work.

What we got was something just across from.the 82d C.P.—a regular two-story house with four bedrooms and two bathrooms, plus a washroom and john and two nice rooms in the basement that could be used for bedrooms or game rooms. I like the two large living room areas, one with a bow front that's all windows, plus a little room for my office and an awning-covered patio. The furniture was bad, but we were told we could requisition what we needed.

I was assigned a lieutenant—a crazy Irishman—and we went out to get furnishings for our new home and for the clubs. We'd go to a promising house and ask to look about. Sometimes I'd make a list in my head of the things there that I wanted and write it down when we got back to the jeep. Later, when we picked up the stuff, we'd give the Germans forms from Military Government looking very official with six signatures.

We did ask if they could spare things like beds. Some were furious, some cried; but most were very nice about it, expecting to get the stuff back one day. Of that I'm not sure, though I understand they are to be reimbursed somehow by Military Government.

❧

Thinking about this whole process today, I'm aghast at what we did; especially when I try to imagine what it would be like if someone came to my door and did the same. But that's what war does to values. We'd won and were top dogs. This was the beginning of my sensing a German trait: these people seemed to look up to and accept authority without rebellion. This made me realize in another way the kind of maverick I seem to be, given my German background.

August 8 (continued)
We can't drink the water here unless it's treated, for supplies are badly polluted. And we don't have hot water as yet. We have two gas heaters, but the pressure isn't high enough; so the division has promised to find an electric heater and install it for us, along with an electric stove. Last night Little Vi and I drove about four miles over to Captain Brooks's apartment to take a bath.

Some sections of Berlin smell because of the dead bodies buried in the wreckage. Yesterday over at the C.P. I saw them loading long covered things on a wagon, and the MP there said they had just found five bodies in a bomb shelter behind the house. Some said it isn't uncommon for Germans here to commit suicide when they're turned out of their homes.

One night a lieutenant from the 325th regiment and I drove over to the British and Russian zones. We saw the Brandenburg Gate which is badly pockmarked. Along the way, like big billboards, are huge pictures of Roosevelt, Stalin, and other bigwigs. It's queer; on our side of the canal the buildings are bombed but habitable in spots. On the Russian side—like along the Unter den Linden— things seem just leveled; and that's the heart of Berlin. It's a scene of desolation.

There's a terrific black market in the *tiergarten* around the Brandenburg Gate. Our guys are making thousands of dollars apiece selling cigarettes and rations to the Russians. Cigarettes now go for ten to fifteen dollars a pack (they used to get a hundred dollars, I'm told), ten-in-one rations now go for hundreds of dollars, and wristwatches (which seem to be a real novelty) bring prices in the thousands. Those with the loudest tick and black faces or sweep hands seem to intrigue them most, so $2.98 Mickey Mouse watches are in great demand—and of course the Air Corps is flying them in!

You might wonder where the Russians get this kind of money. We heard that they'd not been paid for three years or more and that some deal was made by a U.S. general to give them back pay in the same kind of occupation money we use. Theirs has a dash in front of the serial number to show it's Russian, but it's accepted by us as legal tender. I imagine Russians are smart enough to know the money won't be any good once they get home, so they barter for stuff they *can* take home, like watches.

Last night we attended the opening of the Press Club. It's in a large residence, beautifully done up. We met war correspondents—U.S., Danish, Canadian—and even got to chat with Jack Benny, Ingrid Bergman, harmonica virtuoso Larry Adler, and Martha Tilton, who sang with Benny Goodman. Pictures were being shot all over the place. Larry played the piano for us, and a bunch of us sang, and it was gay and exciting. Jack Benny is older looking than I expected and had few wisecracks. Guess he must be a script man. Ingrid looks just like a lovely country girl and speaks with an accent one notices less on the screen. I was amused when she combed her hair at the dinner table!

General Gavin wanted us to meet all the troop trains as the division arrived, and this is a beautiful example of all the SNAFUs one contends with in the military. On Sunday night we heard that the first train was coming in on Monday afternoon at two o'clock. Monday morning we went to Berlin District Headquarters Command to get equipment, since ours hadn't yet arrived. I had to get an OK from no less than a general and sign my life away to get three field ranges, two thirty-two-gallon GI cans, and three aluminum twenty-gallon pots to make coffee at the depot.

Then I had to break into the RC warehouse to get supplies, for I'd forgotten the keys. The building they'd given us after kicking out the Germans had been taken over again by the Germans through some misunderstanding. We had to remove them the second time and place another lock so they couldn't return.

While I waited for a jeep to haul the stuff, I took the car to the motor pool to have the oil changed. They also took off the muffler for a necessary welding job, but I couldn't wait. So I drove off with the car sounding like a halftrack, attracting plenty of attention—only to learn that the train wouldn't be in till four o'clock the next morning!

I spent an hour finding a spot to leave the equipment and supplies where they'd be safe. Then I had to make arrangements to get donuts and get the muffler put back on before the 4:00 A.M. deadline—when they got hold of me to say the train would be in at six at another station. So I got a truck and some GIs to move our supplies. After being misdirected and having to come back for new directions, we finally got the stoves up and water on, only to find out the trains would probably be in at ten that evening. Went back to the station at 9:30 and kept water hot till past midnight. At 12:30 we were told there'd be no train that night. Went out in the morning at ten. It came in at noon.

I'm sure I've missed a couple of dozen little things that came up along the way—like commandeering a jeep, tearing off to get donuts, and getting picked up for speeding—but it was worth it when the men filed off the train with the band blaring out the division's "All American Song." Part of it goes like this:

> We're All American and proud to be
> For we are the soldiers of liberty.
> Some ride the gliders through the enemy,

Others are sky paratroopers.
We're All American, and fight we will
Till all the guns of the foe are still,
Airborne, from skies of blue
We're coming through.
Take your jumps, take your bumps, let's go!
  INTERLUDE
Put on your boots—your parachutes,
Get all those gliders ready to attack today;
For we'll be gone—into the dawn
To fight 'em all the 82d way—Yea! [Repeat Chorus]

It's a real snappy tune and gives you a lump in your throat, no kidding. And the guys were all so glad to see us and hungry after five to seven days traveling in the small forty-and-eight boxcars.

General Gavin told me later that he and his Russian interpeter had flown around all morning trying to locate the trains, which the Russians had stopped and run onto an unused track. It turned out, though, that all that particular day they had been right here in Berlin being switched around.

After we had served one train, they told us all the other trains would come in at Templehof Station, about eight miles from where we were. One train was already in in fact, and we had to pick up stoves and all and hustle. Now they've installed radio communication from a station just outside of Berlin which notifies us when a troop train passes there, and we have the boys at the station keeping water hot from the time it's supposed to arrive. They call at the house to alert us. But even that doesn't work; for we were called at 11:30 two nights ago, went out in pouring rain, and waited till 1:30 A.M. when General Gavin radioed out to send us home. Then the phone got me out of bed at 4:30 saying the train would be in at 5:00 A.M. It's really hectic. We've now served seven trains and have five to go. Wish they could all come in at once and get it over.

We went out to Templehof Airdrome yesterday to see General Ike and Field Marshall Georgi Konstantinovich

Zhukov come in. Zhukov took a prominent part in the Battle of Stalingrad, relief of Leningrad, and capture of Berlin and was the first Soviet military man to get a high political post. He's a rather short man with a pouter-pigeon front entirely covered with medals!

This was the first time I'd seen the honor guard from the 325th Parachute Infantry Regiment—three platoons of guys all over six feet tall with white scarves, white belts, white laces in their jump boots, and shiny plated bayonets. They're specially picked and trained in military precision and rifle drill; it's thrilling to watch them perform. Troopers are, without a doubt, the tops! Their pride shines through, and you never see one who looks sloppy.

Now that the men are arriving, we have to hurry to get the clubs ready. We eat at a new officers' mess in a lovely house near here. Besides German waitresses, there's a trained German butler who makes it seem anything but an Army mess. If he sees you take out a cigarette, he's at your elbow to light it. Your coffee cup is always filled.

Got two new gals today, and two arrive tomorrow, so I've had the fellows here setting up beds, getting sheets from the warehouse, and bringing in coal to heat water for our laundry. We still don't have our electric water heater, and there's a story that the Germans are pleading for us not to turn the gas on for fear there will be a large number of suicides.

So, in addition to using the facilities at Captain Brooks's apartment, we've been offered use of the private bath of the chief of staff (all marble with glassed-in shower) and even the bath in General Gavin's house. Hear my water boiling on the little double-burner Coleman stove Ed Brooks brought us. Guess I'll wash my hair.

10A Kaiser Wilhelm Strasse, Steglitz, Berlin, September 5, 1945

Our own Dottie and Louise opened the 504 Club last Thursday, our fourth. Dotty is short, with a long, dark pageboy bob, and eyes and eyelashes that make men swoon when she looks up and flickers them. She reminds me of Deanna Durbin, and is just as nice as she is sweet, always with things to say in a spilling-out enthusiasm. She's from Dillon, Montana, and did radio work in New York City before she joined American Red Cross. Louise, a teacher from St. Paul, is about my height, with lovely, naturally wavy auburn hair. She's a beautiful, almost stately gal with a warm smile that makes men immediately feel at home. Today at chow we reminisced about Minnesota and State Fair time in the autumn around Labor Day.

Their club is the largest in Berlin. It was a well-known restaurant with a large lounge, an orchestra box and stage, an attractive cafe room that they've done over in Tyrolean style, a huge outdoor dance floor with tables under blue and yellow umbrellas, and lattice fences covered with vines surrounding it all. Upstairs there are writing rooms, a library, game rooms, and some where they have classes in German and Russian which I hope to attend. An artist sketches GIs each evening. There's always an orchestra or something special, and often dancing. Trained staff serve the boys at the tables so they don't have to sweat out lines. Hours are from ten to ten, and there's a huge breakfast crowd. Louise said they've already had Russians drop in, some bringing bottles of vodka and demanding glasses. It's hard to explain to them that we don't allow liquor in our clubs.

At the formal opening it was named the Franklin Delano Roosevelt Club. A cable to Eleanor asking permission had received the answer "No permission needed. Grateful for tribute." The evening was a great success with ceremonies on the outdoor Tyrolean Terrace. Colonel Tucker, commander of 504th Parachute Infantry Regiment, presented a big key to a GI, and General Gavin poured champagne for the two boys who had submitted the name. Photographers milled about to record the event.

Close by in the same neighborhood is our officers' club in a big white house with wide steps leading up to the main entrance. The biggest attraction is on the second floor. In a large room, on a table about as big as the room itself, a miniature countryside is laid out with villages, railroad tracks and depots, and of course elecric trains as only the Germans can build them. The guys look like happy little kids when they get involved, instead of 82d Airborne officers.

Little Vi opened the 325 Glider Infantry Club on Saturday. She's a cute girl from Indianapolis, with a naturally curly short bob and a crooked-tooth grim. For quite some time we couldn't find a suitable building in Vi's area; too many were either bombed out or not large enough. Finally we took over an old school building that had little plaster left on the walls and was in awful shape. But the regiment got German contractors to rip out walls, replaster the whole place, paint everything, and work miracles. Little Vi's managing it alone, so I helped her a lot. She's called it the Let's Go Inn.

Stevie (the gal who married Major Piper in Epinal) opened her 505 Parachute Infantry Regiment Club the same night. She's the one I was with in Germany when we followed the 82d up to Ludwigslust. Stevie's from Oak Park, Illinois, and one of those people you run into once in a while who are tops in every way—good to look at and to be with in a wholesome, healthy way. Two of the new girls are working with her.

When we were looking for a place in the 505 area, we found one lovely home, but it was not quite large enough. So we went to the next one thinking we might take over both. The woman pointed to a sign in the yard, "Off Limits to Military Personnel," signed by Military Government. We thought there was something fishy about it, so we went to check it out. The military Government was located in the next block in a lovely old place with fifty-some rooms and glory be, it was getting ready to move, so we requisitioned the building and got it. It's a dream of a place with beautiful furniture, paintings, art objects, a barber shop, shoeshine room, tailor shop, and sketch room complete with an art instructor. On opening night, even though a couple of fuses blew, we walked into the most charming atmosphere: a string quartet from the Berlin Symphony was playing by candlelight. The club got the name Mittlehof Manor, and does give the feeling of top drawer! We never did learn why the nearby house was off limits.

Glenna, my Berchtesgaden trip friend, who comes from Denver, has been a ballet dancer and is a published writer, opened her club in the Divarty (Division Artillery) area yesterday afternoon. It's in a huge residence that used to belong to a well-known physicist. It has one room two stories high that had had some huge equipment in it, a wonderful dark room, and former laboratory rooms with lots of windows. The place had been bombed, but because the German scientist was a friend of the Russians, they repaired and redecorated it. Now it's in wonderful shape for us.

When the Russinas left it, they took the man, his family, and all the furniture, so we had to completely refurnish it. It has lovely balconies, round alcoves at the corners of the front rooms, a large well-kept lawn with a fountain where Glenna has put lawn furniture. She invited ATS (British WACs) and had a marvelous band for a tea dance, and served chocolate-frosted donuts, ice cream, and coffee. This is the Crown Prince Club.

As I told you, I'm senior club director for all the 82d clubs, and help with the big central Titania Palast for everyone in Berlin and another small club out at Templehof Airdrome which is open all day to serve people coming in or waiting for planes. I no longer have to do all the bookkeeping; each club director is getting her own revolving fund, which takes that off my hands. It's less complicated now because we don't have to charge at snack bars here, and I've turned over all supplies, which were such a terrible responsibility to keep straight, to the Berlin District ARC warehouse. So I don't have that to worry about either.

My job, after getting the regimental clubs set up and operating, is to see that the gals get their reports in, are

helped with their books, and get equipment they need; I
oversee programming, convey all their requests to Harry
Ratliff, our ARC boss here, and do what I can to make their
work easier. As a result, most of my time is spent driving
around Berlin in the Chrysler, and I now know my way
pretty well.

Smashed our car up a bit about ten days ago. It was one
of those hectic days. I'd finally arranged for a detail to go
pick up some furniture I'd requisitioned for our house. But
the trucks didn't come till 4:15, too late to go for the furniture, so I decided to use them instead to clean out our
warehouse. We loaded eight field range cabinets on one
truck to go to Quartermaster, and put the stoves and kettles I'd borrowed on the other to be returned to Berlin District. We were hurrying to get there by five, with me leading
the trucks, when all of a sudden the whole line of traffic
stopped right now! I didn't even have time to get my foot
on the brake, and smashed into the little civilian car ahead
of me, puncturing the square exposed gas tank on the rear.
With his gas running out all over the street, the Russian
driver was throwing his arms in the air and yelling like a
wild man. I've now seen a "mad Russian" and it was scary.

Traffic stopped. Quite a crowd gathered. A news correspondent from the *New York Times*, whom I'd met at the
Press Club, came up and took charge, telling me to stay
away from the Russian. I leaned later that the Russians
pay through the nose for a gallon of gas, let alone wondering how he got the car in the first place. I tried to put myself in his place. Then my good friend Captain Brooks just
happened along. He and the correspondent got our car
towed to ordnance, and he took me home. Just banged my
knee a bit, nothing serious, and the car is in shape again
though minus some of its chrome. Of course I've taken
more than my share of razzing.

The 325 officers had a regimental dance about ten days
ago. They have a lovely building if it doesn't rain; for the
roof is partly gone in places and full of holes in others. At
the Titania Palast, the big theater club, we've even had

Russians performing their Cossack dances to that great minor-key music. Since I'm not in charge of a club, my job is more nine to five, so it's easier for me to attend various things in the evening.

Berlin, September 12, 1945

I haven't told you about my big thrill two weeks ago. Came home about 4:35 to find a message: "You have a dinner engagement you wouldn't want to miss. Be at the Midway Club by five." At the time I was in battle dress— slacks and Eisenhower jacket. I called to find out particulars and learned it was dinner at General Eisenhower's and that they'd wait for me. Well! I'd seen him as he flew in at Templehof and figured I might be lucky enough to see him sometime from one end of a long banquet table or something—but not this! So I jumped into my summer uniform and took off.

When I arrived at Midway, the two other gals were wearing civvies! "But wait," they said, "we'll fix you up," and one of them fitted me out in a chic rose-colored suit. We were picked up by Ike's aide and driven to his home, over a causeway on an island in the Wannsee. The driver said the large modern structure had been the home of a Japanese collaborator.

We entered the living room to join a chummy little group consisting of General Eisenhower (five stars) General Lucius Clay (three stars, and who is about second in command here) and another general (one star). Ike said, "I feel I should get down on my knees to you. It's the first time I've seen three American gals in civilian clothes in a long time!" We sat and talked, first over Scotch-and-soda and wonderful cavier. Ike said, "General Zhukov keeps sending caviar all the time, and I'm getting tired of it!"

The house is impressive, sparsely but beautifully furnished in modern decor. It sits up on a hill. From one whole glass wall of the living room there's a lovely view over a flagged terrace with a huge fountain, and a long, long slope down to the lakeshore.

We walked down to the lake and went for a short ride in a big launch. Returning to the house, we were impressed with the guards around the place, especially the two by the expansive windows who reminded me of the ceremony at the Tomb of the Unknown soldier: they would pace across, stop, do an about-face, and pace back. Of course they're sharp 82d troopers!

We went back to the living room. Ike is a warm person— a wonderful conversationalist with a great sense of humor, and a relaxed way of making you feel very much at home. I couldn't help thinking that though we'd been at General Gavin's many times, I still didn't feel as comfortable there as we did immediately with General Eisenhower.

I sat on a sofa beside Ike for a little musicale before dinner. First was a little accordionist in a slinky gown; General Clay had seen her somewhere and thought Ike would like her. I'd heard another officer kidding Lucius that he'd been drunk and hadn't known what he was doing, so I guess he was sweating out her performance a bit, but she was cute and good. Then a huge gal in a blue taffeta formal came out to sing. Her soprano voice wasn't all that great, and she surely wasn't glamourous. Ike leaned over to me and whispered his disapproval. But following her was an excellent violinist, and then the accordion player came back.

Ike asked whether she knew the "Beer Barrel Polka," and when she played it I got the biggest kick out of Ike. He bounced up and down, slapping his knee in time to the music, with a big grin: "That's my regiment's old marching song!" Everyone had to agree with General Clay that his choice was the hit of the evening.

Dinner was announced. The table was lovely with silver and stemware. Wine was served with each course and finally champagne with dessert. After dinner the aide announced coffee in the Ivory Room—a long room thickly carpeted in beige, the walls lined with indirectly lighted niches filled with carved ivory figurines—but Ike said,

"Think I'd rather have it around the fire." That was in a small room with blue-and-white-striped damask covering the walls, with drapes to match. Here the niches enclosed Dresden china figurines. We had coffee and liqueur and a wonderful relaxed conversation. Ike recounted many of his war experiences and reactions—things we'd wondered about, like the 17th Airborne jump over the Rhine when I was with them. When I mentioned this, Ike said "I remember that jump well," he said. "They told me I'd have ninety-some percent glider casualties if I went in as I'd planned. But it was something I felt we had to do. I walked the floor that whole night trying to decide."

He told about his recent trip to Russia and his experiences with the Soviets. "They're so used to jumping at orders from above. If I get a wire when Zhukov is in my office, I often just casually push it aside and go on with the conversation. Zhukov can hardly stand it and sits and squirms and wants to push me into action." He said he tried to be frank with the Russians, but there are certain customs we have and things we do that he felt he never could make them understand.

We talked about movie stars—of those he'd met over there, Ike thought Herbert Marshall and Madeleine Carroll were tops. He liked Bing Crosby too; but most of the rest didn't impress him much. And we talked about uniforms. Ike had gotten a kick out of our guys with their white shoelaces and felt that such things give individuals special pride and are really good for esprit de corps. "Take me, for instance. I like wearing a different tie, and you know I had the dress blouse cut off into what they now call the Eisenhower jacket." Caught up in this, I nearly got General Gavin in a jam. I said, "But wait, general, till you see the 82d's cherry berries!" Immediately he came alive and said, "What's that? What's that?" So I explained that since it was the practice for paratroopers of other countries to wear berets, the 82d was thinking about it and already had the guards at the division C.P. wearing maroon berets they called "cherry berries." Ike thought a minute: "Don't think I'd like that idea very much." I was coached later never to let on to General Gavin that I'd mentioned it.

The finale came when Lucius Clay said he'd take me home, since he lives in our area, and Ike told us to use his sedan and driver. You should see that limo! It's the longest, shiniest black job with five stars on a red plate front and back and little flags flying on the bumpers when the general's in the car.

Little Vi was saying goodnight to her date as we drove up to 10-A Kaiser Wilhelm Strasse. "We just couldn't believe our eyes when that limo drove up! And when you got out in the lovely rose-colored suit we were really floored." Later I had them all, including a colonel and a major, sitting around asking questions and listening to the fairytale story.

Just wrote Ike an informal note. The other day when I was out at the 505 Club, a little old German fellow came in and showed me his identity card, which carried the name of Eisenhower; he thinks Ike may be the son of one of his brothers who went to the States and wanted to know how he could get to see our general. When I told him it would be difficult, he produced a letter he'd written. I promised to send it to Eisenhower, which I've done.

Mittelhof Manor had a dance with U.S. WACs and British ATs gals. The 325 Regimental Jumpmasters played. Although the GIs can fraternize with German frauleins, who are allowed in their beer halls, we're not allowing them, or liquor, in our clubs as yet, by orders from above. I've not seen many WACs, and I don't like stories that go around about them. When I was in the WAAC back home, we had those stories to fight too; and all I knew was the OK situation where I was.

We have lots of parades, but there was a big one a couple of days ago on the eight-lane parkway Tiergarten, between the Brandenburg Gate and the big column, with troops, tanks, and bands from the Russians, British, French, and us. General Patton was here to replace Eisenhower, and

Zhukov was dripping with medals as usual. You may see pictures of it in newsreels or magazines. Margaret Bourke White was there, along with lots of other photographers. Even more exciting shows are those the 82d has been putting on for all the big shots out at Templehof Airdrome. First, about a third of the division passes in review, marching to the band. They're all spiffed up in their white scarves and white gloves and are really sharp, carrying the right flags for all the generals in attendance. Immediately after that, four planes towing gliders come over the field. The gliders cut loose, peel off, and maneuver beautifully, stopping right in a row on the field. The crews jump out and open the noses, and out of two come motorcycles. Out of the others, two jeeps, with chronium hubcaps and white walled tires. As they pass in review, you realize there are six planes overhead, and the fellows start bailing out. What a sight against a clear blue sky, with the camouflaged chutes of the jumpers and the red, yellow, and blue of the equipment or cargo chutes. On an early jump they did for Marshal Zhukov, one man was killed outright when his chute got mixed up with a cargo chute and he landed on his head. Two have died of injuries since, so there's a lot of controversy about continuing. These shows are thrilling, though, and when the band breaks into the "All American" that big lump forms in your throat. As the flag at the head of each group passes, everyone, including spectators, snaps to attention and salutes. As the general's flag dips, it gets to you in a kind of pseudo-patriotism, or is it real?

The last three Saturdays there have been football games out at the impressive stadium. It's the real McCoy, you know; built for the Summer Olympics held here in 1936, when Hitler was still around. Actually, it seemed like back in the States, with masses of traffic around the stadium, crowds of people and exciting games. Halftime performances of the band and the honor guard company are great. A cannon goes off, and they set off camouflage flares, and the company comes marching through a big cloud of green smoke. I'd give anything if you could see it.

The company drills with so much precision and pizzazz, the crowd gasps and then yells and cheers. Four generals, including Ike, say it's the best they've ever seen.

Another great part of the entertainment is watching the Russian soldiers watching the game. Apparently they don't understand the rules, so they spend a lot of time watching the spectators make fools of themselves. I keep trying to figure out their deadpan expressions and keep wondering what's going on in their noggins.

Another big event in the Olympic stadium was an international track meet. It was supposed to be between us, the British, French, and Russians, but it seems the Russians wanted to send back to Moscow for their best athletes. When this was verboten, they pulled out. Even without them, it was like a mini-Olympics. Then, too, there were division reviews at which the 82d received Belgian and Dutch *fourragères*—bright-colored braided cords worn from the shoulder around the top of the sleeve. Supposedly you get them to show that a group has already received a designated number of medals, but I understand that some have never been given to anyone but royalty before. Now there's talk of a French one, and everyone's kidding about where they're going to wear it, since they have one on each arm already! We're close to the most decorated division in history!

13 Sent Back for Reassignment

We hadn't been in Berlin a couple of months when the rumors started flying. Because we felt a closer tie to 82d than we did to ARC, we'd become intimately involved. We'd get to wondering about the future when the news would die down and we'd get on with our programs, only to be upset again later.

Berlin, Germany, September 20, 1945
Rumors have it that the 82d is on its way back to the States, though they don't know whether Category 2 or 4. Four means deactivation and could take them back on November 11 (just rumors); two is strategic reserve, in which case they might leave Berlin but stay on the continent for a month or more. So we're sweating it out again, after thinking we were settled for the winter. We gals are really supposed to stay here no matter what happens, as ARC is operating now, but General Gavin has gotten headquarters to say that if we want to go with the division, we can. It will be a big decision; we're comfortable here and have some great clubs, but we also hate to think of having some other division to work for instead of the good old 82d. So we'll just have to wait and see.

I've been spending much of my time with Bob, a lieutenant in the 325th Glider Infantry. He's a six-four handsome blond and a super dancer, and since I have evenings pretty much off, it's easy to find a dance floor. If I don't know a step, Bob teaches it to me. Sometimes when there aren't many dancing, Bob'll request a Viennese waltz, so we can have the whole floor to ourselves to swoop around.

The night they opened the new Headquarters Club, I

came in late from duty somewhere. As I joined the group at
our table, they said, "We've got a new drink, Vi, a C&B.
Three are guaranteed to put anyone under the table." I
laughed and said, "I've never been drunk. I can hold my liquor and keep up with the crowd." But after I'd finished
only one tall champagne and benedictine, I was out
waltzing with Bob and came back to the table still going in
circles. Heard later that any time you mix hard liquor with
champagne, watch out!

One great party was Sadie Hawkins Day at the Division
Officers' Club. The invitations said, "Dogpatch, Berlin, 3
September 1945, from Marryin' Sam" (alias our chief of
staff) and were addressed to "Eligibul Bachler Fellers, Sub-
ject: Matrimony," adding, "No 98-cent weddins allowed.
Cheek-to-cheek dancin only afta weddins. Race gurunteed
to be demmycratic. Hangin if u don show up will be at
dawn."

But I was telling you about Bob. Our dancing is beginning to draw comments from the onlookers. In addition,
we have lots more in common it seems. We both love to
sing. Bob plays the piano beautifully and announces himself when he comes to pick me up for a date by sitting
down at the piano in our house. (Yes, I requisitioned it with
him in mind!) He loves sports, too. And Bob's unusual in
that he lays everything out on the table. One knows where
she stands! I'm older, so we've decided there'll be nothing
finally serious in our relationship, but we have such great
times that we see each other whenever we can.

Bob loves motorcycles and has one he picked up along
the way somewhere; if the division moves, he has a deal
with the kitchen crew to pack it with their equipment. He
drives it over to the house, and then we usually use the
Chrysler—though once when the Chrysler had a flat we
went out on Bob's motorcycle after a rain, and it was really scary rounding corners on wet cobblestones. Tomorrow
will be a typical Sunday; he's coming over at nine and
we're driving to Neuenhayendorf (new-something village),
outside the Berlin Ring in the Russian zone. To get there

you have to drive through the French sector, and then come to the Russian guards at the Berlin Ring. Bob speaks fluent German but doesn't use it when he explains that we want to go visit relatives in the village. Sometimes we breeze right through; sometimes it takes some talking. But we always make it and get back.

The "relatives" we are going to see tomorrow are a German doctor and his family who sheltered a Jewish doctor who later escaped the Gestapo and got to the States. When Bob's dad, who is a doctor in the Cleveland area, met the Jewish doc and learned he wanted to do what he could for his benefactor and family, he told him he had a son stationed in Berlin, and they made a deal to use Bob as a go-between. A Cleveland group sends lots of small packages to Bob containing bars of soap, sardines, and other canned food, and each Sunday when we can we go over and play Santa. Indeed it is just that. They're like small children, eager and thrilled, and always insist on feeding hungry Bob with whatever they have, maybe *pfefferkuchen* made without shortening. And there's always a present for me to bring home—an egg, a piece of fruit, or something from their garden. Sometimes I take along some Red Cross donuts, which are treasured because they've been cooked in fat, something Germans crave but can't get. They're a great family, and in listening to their stories I'm impressed with the absence of whining or complaining. It almost makes one feel guilty for all we have—mostly our freedom!

Berlin, October 25, 1945

Rumors are rampant. The moving date has gone forward and back so many times, I refuse to listen. Had a big disappointment last week. Bob had gotten a leave to Switzerland, and the division was going to fix it so I could go along. We were excited about driving our car down to Mulhouse to join a tour from there. But at the last minute, for fear the moving date might be moved up, all leaves were canceled. One rumor is that the 82d may be here till January, but more often we hear that it will leave here between the fifth and fifteenth of November and ship in December; though today once again they said the shipping date was moved back to the 12th of December. Shades of Spanhoe! All this uncertainty is made even worse because Christmas is coming up—a time when you want to be with family, and if we can't be Stateside, all of us would like to be with our 82d family. We're opening two more clubs—one for Negros (have two black gals up here now) and a larger one at Templehof Airdrome. They've moved it into a new hangar with huge glass windows overlooking the runways. Planes come in under roof.

Berlin, November 25, 1945

It's finally final! Once more these farewells! Seems the division's to be sent back to an assembly area near Sissone for a couple of weeks before going to a port of embarkation. If that's so, it seems silly for us to go along, though Harry, our Berlin District ARC boss, has promised he'll fly us down to see them off.

Advance groups for the 78th Infantry Division, which is to take over here, have come in. They seem to be pretty good people, but they aren't 82d All Americans! And another thing—we'd always thought the 82d would be sent down to the Bavarian Alps—something I've dreamed about.

❧

One of the last parties was a headquarters prop-blast for Marlene Dietrich. As I mentioned back in France, she was great—no prima donna, just one of the family. That evening she was in a flowing beige chiffon gown and danced all evening with grace and good nature, even though the guys cut in unmercifully. I wonder how many could go home to say, "I danced with Dietrich."

She was in Berlin to be with her terminally ill mother, and I can admit now that I had been the official go-between, used by someone in the United States to pass on food and special supplies to her German mother. Marlene often ate at our mess, and after her mother died, her daughter came to chow with her, wearing an olive drab skirt and Eisenhower jacket. She was a CAT, Civilian Actress Technician, chubby, braids wrapped around her head, nothing like the glamourous person who was later to become a TV personality. Now, years later this very daughter has written a book about her mother which paints an entirely opposite picture of Marlene as a selfish, sex-driven woman. True, she may have stopped by 82d Airborne Divison as often as she did to see General Gavin, but it wasn't entirely selfish, as many a GI who talked or danced with her will attest.

As the 82d prepared to leave, so did Harry Ratliffe, who was also returning to the States. His replacement was to be coordinator of all ARC field work in Berlin. It was then that I changed my mind about going down just to see the 82d off. Harry didn't have to do things by the book. He knew how much 82d meant to me and signed papers for a two weeks' leave to Switzerland, since Bob had cooked up a deal with his CO to drive with me to the 82d assembly area near Sissone instead of going with his company. Just in case, I also had orders from the division "for the purpose of permanent change of station." The same day I got those orders I had the following letter from Miriam Fay, head of the whole ARC show in the European Theater, who had been the boss in England when I was there.

I was very pleased to find upon my arrival in Wiesbaden that you were stationed in Berlin, and hope that it has been an enjoyable assignment for you. It had been my plan to visit there before now, but the pressure of work here at Headquarters has seriously interfered with my field trips. However, I am sending you an excellent representative as our Club Supervisor in Berlin, to take Mr. Ratliff's place of club matters. You will find Miss Alden a splendid person to work with and I know that you will give her every cooperation.

I have not been able to determine exactly what your duties as Senior Club Director are, since that is a new title to me; but Miss Alden will sit down with you and go over the whole picture, and between the two of you I know that you can arrange the work so that everything is adequately taken care of. I have already told her

that you were one of the best business women we ever had in the
Field Club Department, and will be of help to her in keeping her
own bank account straight!

Looking back now, I can see that with the 82d Airborne
leaving and 78th Infantry taking over, this was just about the
worst possible time for me to be away. But the old 82d feeling
was gone, and even though Miriam had said the new club
supervisor was a "splendid person," I remembered having
already worked with her—she was in charge of supplies
when I was with 17th Airborne—and we'd had a couple of
real fights. I could imagine her reaction as Miriam told her
that I might help balance her checkbook!

Then, in addition to Miss Alden, there was to be someone
else on top to coordinate all the ARC activities. So after having run the whole show by myself, now there would be two
higher layers of supervision, and they wouldn't be a General
Gavin and Colonel Ireland. Most important of all, there was
that "something" I really wanted to do, and I was willing to
take any consequences.

When Comer arrived, I told him I was leaving a week
later. I had Harry's signed orders, so there was nothing he
could say or do. Miss Alden was to come in on Thursday; I
would have that afternoon and evening to clue her in on the
whole operation, which was becoming more complicated by
the minute: one club to close; two new ones opening, six
new girls coming in for assignment and billeting. Then when
I heard she wouldn't be in until late Friday, I stayed up all
night typing five single-spaced pages of instructions for the
new supervisor—background on each club with its personnel, those in transition, new personnel to arrive, jeeps and
details, accounting procedures, uniforms, weekly reports
and program, and new girls' housing—plus three pages list-
ing all the billets.

Thinking of this now, it seems out of character for me to
have been downright irresponsible. I probably well deserved
what happened when I returned. But at that point the trip
with Bob was most important, and I didn't care about the

consequences. We decided to go via Brussels and took off in the Chrysler. I wrote home about the trip after it was over and was awaiting reassignment in Wiesbaden.

Wiesbaden, Germany, December 18, 1945
Early on Friday morning, November 16, I was to have had coffee ready when Bob got there, but my alarm hadn't gone off, so he made coffee while I got ready. Then it seemed the car wasn't ready either, for about thirty miles out in Russian territory we had a flat tire. Bob got out to find that the spare was also flat, and we had no pump. He told me to lock myself in while he investigated some buildings we'd passed a way back, strapping on his 45 as he left.

We were lucky; the buildings turned out to be some kind of Russian motor pool. They wouldn't let Bob take their pump; we had to drive back on the flat, but in about an hour we were fixed up. Bob had quite a time with two Russians who spoke German, and one even some English. We gave them each a big Hershey bar, and they seemed quite happy.

About twenty-five miles farther on we came to a funny intersection and found out from some Germans that we were driving around the Berlin Ring and had missed the one exit that would have taken us to the *reichsautabahn*— the only way we could get through Russian territory. We were where we weren't supposed to be and had to drive about forty miles back.

Then, before we reached Helmstedt (where the Russian and British territories meet), the oil gauge fell to zero, and we found we had no oil. All we could do was creep along; but we were lucky again. In about eight miles we ran into an ack-ack outfit, where we picked up a new tube, a new jeep tire that would fit the Chrysler, five gallons of oil— and lunch.

Sailing along the autobahn after that was delightful un- til about four-thirty, when we hit an unbelievable wall of fog. I mean just that. We had to inch along until we came

to the first exit, labeled Bielefeld, and Bob remembered it
was to be the first stopover for 82d convoys. How lucky
could we be! We drove in, following taillights around narrow streets, and pulled up at the office of the town may-
or. He told us where to find a British officers' hotel, a
wholly unexpected surprise. Those British officers lived
well. We joined them for a five-course dinner, including
steaks and a bottle of champagne. There was a band and a
good dance floor, which we had much to ourselves. Bob
requested all our favorite waltzes, tangos, and rumbas.
Nor did these Brits seem bothered by having male and female in the same building. Bob was given a room right
next to mine, and there was no one to check whether he
stayed there!

When we left the next morning, the weather was clear,
and it was still a novelty to drive one-way traffic on wide,
beautifully engineered concrete highways. Bob was forever
hungry, and I fed him cookies and candy bars as he drove.
Toward dusk he got sleepy, and I took over. I must have
dropped off, for I smashed the car through a roadblock at a
blown bridge. We didn't go over the edge, but one head-
light was out, and the other was shining up at a weird an-
gle until Bob pried it back into place with a screwdriver.

We had to leave the autobahn and drove through Duren
just about dusk. Not one building was left standing, just a
wall here and there and shreds of trees, all against a dim-
ming sky. It was an eerie sight. Ditto for Aachen after
some rough roads. As we neared the Belgian border, we
were sweating out Bob's orders which were questionable.
We had no trouble, and drove into Liège about 9:30. We
spent one night there and two in Brussels with Madame
Jane Havegnee at Pension Brialmont. This may sound like
the red light district, but a *pension* [pronounced pon-si-
own] is just a kind of boardinghouse in a private home. I
liked Brussels better than Paris, though I was reminded of
the bigger city when I saw the sidewalk *pissoirs*—urinals
enclosed in round metal walls that begin about kneehigh
from the ground, allowing one to see the user's feet and

legs (nobody seems to have been concerned about us women)!

We had a devil of a time finding the assembly area called Camp Oklahoma City, where the Division would be until shipping out for home. It was out in the country near Sissone, and was so large that we had to ask five times before we found E Company. We came into camp on Tuesday night, and I stayed till Saturday noon. I had Thanksgiving dinner with E Company, but otherwise there wasn't much to do; the weather was foul and foggy. Bob's CO didn't give him any duties, though, and covered for him all the while I was there.

Bob arranged with the colonel of the camp to have two GIs who were eligible for furlough to drive with me to Mulhouse, France, where I was to make connections for the Switzerland tour. It was hard to leave Bob, but the parting had to come sometime. Wally, his CO, said E Company would surely miss their Red Cross gal and gave me $50 worth of German marks, which he wouldn't be able to use in the States.

The two PFCs and I left Saturday noon. We drove through my old stomping ground at Châlons-sur-Marne, and got fogged in again about five-thirty just out of Vesoul, I think it was. We decided to spend the night at the next town, stopped an Army truck and got directions to a mess hall. An officer there invited us to a hotel in the little town I wish I could remember the name of; It was a small walled community dating back B.C. they told me. He took me to a dance at their officers' club in an old chateau that loomed up out of the mist as we drove along narrow streets. There was an eleven-piece band with a stubby little leader in heavy glasses and a big POW stenciled across the seat of his baggy gray pants. It was a Herr Louie oompah-oompah band if ever I heard one. Then I spied five 82d patches— fellows who were on temporary duty there. I actually knew one of them, so again it was a totally unexpected storybook time.

[My letter went on to tell about the great experience of

discovering Switzerland in ten days after leaving Mulhouse; and my waiting over to find someone to drive with me to Frankfurt. I left with a major and a captain as passengers.] When we reached Frankfurt at almost ten that evening, who did I run into in the hotel lobby but Bonnie, who'd been Harry Ratliff's secretary. Harry's replacement had fired her, and she'd just left Berlin. "You're not going to like what you find when you get back," she told me. "Comer was furious that you'd taken the car and is royally cleaning house." Besides that, I was going to be a week late getting back—but I'd known I was taking a calculated risk and actually visualized there'd be consequences I might regret. Bonnie said, "Vi, he's a great big BTO!" In your language, that means 'Big Time Operator.'

Next day I picked up a corporal at USFET [U.S. Forces, European Theater] to drive with me to Berlin. He had driven an officer to Frankfurt and I sympathized when he told how they'd gotten lost in the fog on the autobahn, and all of a sudden found an eight-foot gap in the road with a drop I forget how deep. He said, "Instinctively, I stepped on the gas and we jumped the gap, but we sheared off the rear wheels." When I recounted Bob's and my all-too-similar experience, we truly felt like companions in misery!

We hit snow not too far out, and the road was slick and icy the whole two hundred miles. Our Chrysler didn't have a working heater, but neither had the jeeps we'd lived with for years. After getting lost in the fog once, we decided to spend the night in Braunschweig and go on to Berlin the next day.

❧

The rest of my letter home didn't tell everything that happened, for I wasn't exactly proud of that experience. I dropped off my passenger the next afternoon and got home to Kaiser Wilhelm Strasse about two-thirty on December fifth. When Louise and Little Vi saw the car, they rushed out and threw their arms around me. "You'll never know what it's been like these past weeks. Over and over again we kept saying that this couldn't happen if Vi were here!" As we mounted the steps the three German women who worked for us were waiting: They cried and said "We've been waiting, and brought all these Christmas decorations so we'd be ready for your homecoming. We wanted you to know how we celebrate."

Over Scotch and coffee, Little Vi and Louise poured out all that had happened. Their angry words were still flooding the room when the phone rang. It was Helen, director of our officers' club; when she found I was home, she wanted me to come right over and talk. I called Comer to report in and asked whether it would be OK if I came in the following morning. He said he had to confer with the new club supervisor. After several moments the answer came: "We've decided you may come in in the morning. By the way, did you bring the car back? Is it in good condition? I want you to know that we now have a motor pool and will you please turn it in!" I bristled but was not surprised after what Bonnie had told me in Frankfurt.

I had dinner with Helen, and we sat and talked till fourthirty in the morning. It seems each club had had to turn in its vehicles to the new motor pool, and now nobody could get transportation when they wanted it. "He gave us direct orders that there were to be no more meals or cigarettes given to entertainers. Reports are to be in at a deadline or else. We have to fill out papers for every stick of furniture in our club."

Helen added, "you know that in addition to coffee and donuts and Cokes, on my own I started selling super sandwiches the officers loved. He gave me a direct order to stop selling as of right now, and I had $45 worth of food on hand. When all that happened, I was telling it to a colonel from Paris, who said he'd just go ahead selling. So I did, but I sent a wire to Paris headquarters, just to clear myself, only to find out that the direct order had not come from Paris at all as I'd been told. You won't believe this, Vi, but Paris called in the commissioner from Wiesbaden, and as a result Comer and Alden were told if they couldn't handle their jobs they'd be replaced by someone who could. I was actually called in for testimony, with a secretary taking down everything in shorthand."

She went on, "The Monday before, in the midst of all this fracas, we had a meeting of all the 82d club directors and decided to ask Comer just what your job would be. Miss Alden answered and said, 'There'll be plenty of work for both of us. She'll continue as senior club director.' So I wonder what will happen tomorrow. Let me know soon as you find out."

I wondered too, and had my doubts. When I reported in next morning, I was left cooling my heels for nearly half an hour, giving me time to get prepared for what was to come. The gist of it, from Alden: "Had you been here when I arrived, I'm sure we could have divided up the work. Since you weren't, we had to make other arrangements. Now there seems nothing left but for you to report to Wiesbaden for reassignment." I was shocked, but frankly, I couldn't fault her there. In fact, I'd been thinking of asking for just that—a thought that was reinforced by the idea of working with her—but I hated to have them make the decision. I was both angry and hurt, especially when I found out later that Harry's and my names were mud in both Paris and Wiesbaden. Seemed Comer and Alden earlier reported that the ARC situation in Berlin was one terrible mess, whereas in fact a smooth-running organization of happy people had just been turned into a rebellious conniving group bordering on mutiny.

I'm not discounting the fact that had I been there, some of this wouldn't have happened, but I'd have balked all the way at making paper work, regulations and "efficiency" the order of the day when what we were there for was to be caring human beings. As I think of it now, I'm reminded of *M.A.S.H.* and the war in Korea. Comer was a perfect "Frank," picky-picky and ever ready to squeal to higher brass about the shortcomings of others; he even had a "Hot Lips" to back him up.

When the news got out that I was to return to Wiesbaden for reassignment there *was* a minor mutiny among the 82d girls, who'd been waiting for my return so I could be a cushion between them and Comer and help them fight. Helen had actually asked to see him and told him of the loyalty we 82d gals felt toward one another and how the others looked up to me as their "boss." She concluded: "You've just got to keep Vi in Berlin. If nothing else, I'll step down as club director with the officers and let her have my job, and I'll be her program director."

Apparently he was alarmed, for next day he had Miss Alden call me. "It's too bad to have you leave when you know the situation here so well; and even though headquarters expects you for reassignment, I'll take it upon myself to let you stay as senior program director, working with all the clubs." When I said I'd not be interested, she suggested I might like to supervise the donut kitchen! Of course, I refused that too.

With the 82d gone and this new regime, I would have been almost glad to be leaving Berlin if it hadn't been so close to the holidays. Orders were cut for me to leave on a Tuesday the tenth but the devil in me made me go over Comer's head. I called Miriam Fay in Wiesbaden, explaining about all the farewell parties I'd have to cancel, and she said I could report in the following Monday. With a continued defiance, I kept the Chrysler, for I had to scoot all over Berlin saying goodbyes. Comer tried twice to get that car turned in to the pool, but we used it to the end—to haul all my stuff down to the station for the final farewells. What happened to it after that I never found out.

The Berlin Express to Frankfurt and Wiesbaden was comfortable enough, with compartments for two and a diner for all the brass going to and from Berlin. On the way, there was time to think about that past month. I tried switching roles, and decided that Comer and Alden had good cause for what they did; it was the way they did it that made all the difference. For the gang of gals in Berlin, that difference would make being there now anything but the happy family situation we'd known. It reminded me of the Office of Price Administration in Portland, Oregon, and the notes from the old gang that under a new supervisor it wasn't the same—that the happy family feeling was gone, replaced with "everything by the book."

Even seeing things in that light, though, I wouldn't have changed my decision to make the trip with Bob. I had known it was unfair on my part; perhaps Harry Ratliff had too, but he cared about us and was a man of his word. Now I thought of the "consequences" I'd chosen and wondered just what they would be. If there was a Comer type making decisions in Wiesbaden, chances were I could be sent home for insubordination. But in all likelihood it would be Miriam Fay, and I knew I could talk with her.

When I reported in at Wiesbaden and announced who I was, everyone seemed most interested. The Berlin story had been all over headquarters. I was so thankful that Miriam Fay was the one I had to answer to. I respected her and wasn't disappointed. I told her my story and why I had done it, admitting I knew that taking the car was questionable, but it had been given to us and not to a motor pool. I reminded her that she knew I'd kept my nose to the grindstone in England even when I learned that many other gals had taken off to see the country, and that this time it was something I really wanted to do. I pointed out that Harry had given us permission to do it, that I had valid orders, and that even though I was gone an extra week, I had notified Comer when I'd be back and why.

Miriam seemed to understand and said she'd been led to believe I'd been a far worse scoundrel: "The reports didn't sound like Vi at all." I began to feel more comfortable and told her that because the 82d had always thought they'd be sent to Bavaria, I'd dreamed of that and would love an assignment somewhere in the Bavarian mountains.

She said, "I'm not sure of any openings just now, but I do know from experience that you're good around an office. You could be a bonus to us if you'd be willing to help us out while you wait for another assignment." I agreed and recall so well checking reports from clubs and drooling over the ones from Garmisch-Partenkirchen down in Bavaria, envying the girls who were there and trying to picture what it would be like. It was good to have evenings and weekends free with no responsibility for clubs, but somehow it seemed an unhealthy atmosphere. There was too much ARC, too many gripes to listen to.

The first weekend, Miriam's secretary and I were guests at Bad Nauheim, a beautiful little town sixty-seven kilometers from Wiesbaden and headquarters for the fifteenth Army. A big dance was scheduled, but it was canceled because of General Patton's death, since this had been his headquarters. Earlier that week, I had been invited to Bonnie and Shack's wedding. Bonnie, as I said, had been Harry Ratliff's secretary, and Shack was Bob's roommate.

When I got back I wrote to Bob about the wedding, and how much I'd missed having his broad shoulder to cry on during all that had happened in Berlin. Bob understood me better than anyone I'd known; I always knew where I stood with him, and he helped me see things in perspective. I had a long letter from him after he was home in Ohio. He talked a lot about my Berlin troubles and went on: "Vi, I do admire your luck. Somehow I feel that all will be ironed out smoothly for you. Call it a hunch, if you like, but I feel that something big will take place in your life before the year is out."

On the day before Christmas a symphony orchestra and hundred-voice choir did Mozart's *Requiem* in a huge Wiesbaden cathedral, which was jammed. In that appropriately ancient setting, it was truly a religious experience. And Christmas with the 508th Parachute Infantry Regiment was a bit like coming home, since they'd been attached to 82d some time before and wore its famous patch. We danced, and I got a lump in my throat at the rendition of "Stille Nacht" on the E string, with lights out, by a German in the dance band who had been first violinist with the Frankfurt Symphony.

Shortly after the holidays I received an assignment to open a second club at Heidelberg. Once again, I went over the head of the woman who made assignments and talked to Miriam Fay: "I've opened and closed so many clubs, I just can't stand the thought of another." Great gal that she was, she said, "You can opt out of Heidelberg and wait for something else."

About that time there was a conference of all the supervisors of the ETO. One turned out to be Ellie, who'd been with 17th Airborne when our two divisions had been divided up for going home, the gal whose request I'd ignored when she asked my help in getting assigned to 82d Airborne. And here she was, not only an area supervisor but in charge of the area that included Garmisch-Partenkirchen!

I asked her about it, and she said, "Vi, everyone wants to go to Garmisch!" But, she went on, "the club director there is planning to leave in February." Without thinking, I said, "How about my going down and understudying her for a month and then taking over?" Ellie promised to ask Miriam Fay.

I can still see Ellie at a cocktail party two days later, leaning out from where she was sitting at the other end of the room to attract my attention. Holding up her right hand with the thumb and middle finger making a circle, she said, "You leave with me in the morning!"

It was one of those peak experiences I just couldn't believe! From a situation in which I could easily have beeen fired and sent home, I ended up with the prize assignment of the European Theater! I had to write Bob he'd been right! I smiled to myself as I thought of how many times I'd packed all my worldly belongings in a matter of hours!

I was the envy of all the gals at the hotel that night. When I got into bed I felt a bit of guilt but was thankful to Ellie, and thankful too that she never did know I'd not done for her some months before what she'd now done for me. Like the Red Cross accepting me without a degree, I thought, "this is another super charm!" There had been little ones in between, but this was a big one. And they were to keep coming!

PART IV

Occupation Leave Center

14 Bavarian Shangri-la

Headquarters had made sleeper reservations to Munich for Ellie and me, but at 6 P.M. in Frankfurt we found that we'd been bumped by some officers. The GI who had to tell us this was furious. Since we did have the assimilated rank of captain, he said, "The officers that bumped you were only captains too, and pretty damned un-American doing that to a couple of their own women."

So, while Ellie sweated out cancellations, I used my cigarettes for tipping and had a couple of Germans load my footlocker.

We finally did get a berth, and I fell asleep dreaming of Garmisch-Partenkirchen—the Shangri-la of Bavaria's mountains. It was special enough to have been picked for the Winter Olympics of 1936, and now the military had chosen it as a leave center for the whole ETO.

It was snowing heavily when we arrived in Munich. As we were walking through the badly bombed station a big blob of brick and concrete fell just in front of us, reminding us how recently we'd been at war. I stayed at Ellie's apartment and found that her secretary, Jean, and Jean's boyfriend were going to a nearby opera house to see *Hansel and Gretel*. I cried, "Oh, I've always hoped to hear that opera, and how great it would be to hear it right here in Germany." Jean said, "We don't have an extra ticket, Vi, but why not come along and take a chance one will turn up?"

We walked over through the falling snow. Sure enough, near the entrance we found a sergeant who came up about to my shoulder; he had two tickets to the opera and was looking for an American to join him! That's how I met Pete, who said he often came to Garmisch to ski. I invited him to the club I'd not yet seen.

I could have spent New Year's Eve at Ellie's but decided I wanted to get to Garmisch. So on December 31, 1945, Tommy drove me down, and I exclaimed all the way at the fairyland of white trees and chalets top heavy with snow. The mountains got higher and higher as we neared Garmisch, until we were right in the midst of them, with the Zugspitze (the highest peak in Germany) standing guard.

Garmisch-Partenkirchen! If I've used the adjective "picturesque" before, I was wrong; I should have reserved it for this Bavarian town. There were hundreds of chalets and several of the onion-top church steeples that became an emblem of Garmisch for me. Some homes and inns and big hotels had characters and scenes painted on the exterior plaster walls between exposed wooden beams.

The streets were alive with natives in *lederhosen* (the leather shorts with colorful felt suspenders you see in pictures) or Bavarians and GIs with skis or skates over their shoulders, and horse-drawn sleighs with jingling bells adding music to the scene. It was much too much like the movies to seem real!

We stopped at the club, which was in an ultramodern theater building with a circular drive, set back off Bahnhofstrasse (railroad station street). We entered a large lobby. Straight ahead in the center was a theater that seated twelve hundred. Along each side were halls with alphabetized check rooms, called *garderobes*. Those to the left had been made into a small library, a Ping-Pong room, a barbershop, a music room, and two offices. The main part of the club was in the cafe area in the rear, an L-shaped wing with low upholstered booths along outside window walls that overlooked a terrace and lovely park.

We were greeted by Harriet Frost, whose striking white hair matched her name but whose warm smile below bright blue eyes was welcoming. "You're Vi! We've been expecting you. I'll get my coat and head you out to our house. Fay's waiting there."

Number 5 Grassbergstrasse, about a mile from the club and named for the Grassberg (grass mountain) behind it, was to be my new address. We drove along Fruelingstrasse (spring street) through what I found out later is one of the most photographed scenes in Bavaria. The street, barely wide enough for two cars, ran along the Loisach River. On the opposite side was a whole line of chalets—with lace curtains and often red geraniums in the windows—whose second stories overhung the street; often there was washing on a line at the edge of the balcony. From there it was on up a hill to a sprawling modern chalet with long slanting rooflines and narrow second-story balconies across the front and back. A wide driveway on the right led to a double garage. This is where six of us lived. It even had a name: Charlottenhof.

We walked in through a large entrance hall with an adjoining powder room, common in larger homes in Germany. The living room we entered was the homiest I'd seen in Europe. A grand piano beneath a huge oil portrait seemed to hold down the right-hand end of the room. Floor to ceiling windows and French doors covered the entire length on the right, to the sun alcove at the far end, with brightly upholstered sofas beneath the windows. The focal point was a stone fireplace in the center on the left, with two comfy divans reaching out perpendicularly. This was to be the spot for many a party or gabfest or just lounging to watch the fire. We had an intercom system too, with which we could talk with Hedwig, our cook and housekeeper, who had her own room.

The house had been taken over from Frau Furstenburg, a doctor's widow who now lived in an apartment made for her in the double garage. And I might as well tell my guilty story. The second winter I was there we moved her from that garage to another apartment, because we'd had trouble starting our jeeps in the morning and wanted to put them in a heated garage! I felt better when I received a letter from Frau Furstenburg later, saying that the best years of the war and post war for her were when the Red Cross girls lived in her house.

I inherited Fay's room—a Bavarian Hollywood setting, with glassed-in door and windows opening to the balcony and its mountain scenery. These could be covered at night with drapes of the same material that covered the walls and enclosed an alcove in the side wall which contained my built-in bed. A large private bath, done in yellow tile, included a bidet (I'd always smiled at the story of the GIs using a bidet to wash their feet). Topping the Hollywood atmosphere was the fact that my bedroom had a private circular stairway from the living room.

I even had a bedside phone. Ray, a GI electrician, said that since this was a leave center, a lot of brass came to Garmisch, where, according to rank, they might luck out with a lovely chalet, complete with cook and "hot and cold running frauleins"; sometimes he even had to hook up temporary phone lines at their trains. "For some," he said, "I didn't mind. For others I just saw red; and I decided it was even more important for you to have a bedside phone. Just promise me that should there ever be an inspection, you'll hide it under the bed or behind the drapes."

Fay came down to meet me. "How did you pull this off to come down and understudy me? I think it's great, and you can be sure I'll let you take over with me just looking on. Glad you came today; we're open late tonight!" As we were having a drink we were joined by Frenchie, a young girl Fay had brought along from a former club. Frenchie lived with us. With her fluent French and German, and her efficient demeanor, she always knew how to get things done. I even learned a bit of each language from her. We had dinner at a junior officer's home and went to work. The club was open till 1:00 A.M. this New Year's Eve, the last day of 1945, and it was jammed. Since I was new, I just sat and talked with the men enjoying food and drink. We broke the rules about liquor for the evening and had a baby bath filled with "bathtub gin"!

Next morning, breakfast was in our dining room, with its Swedish modern furniture of beautiful inlaid wood. We ate off Royal Meissen—the onion pattern set was our everyday china! The food was serve-yourself from a large lazy susan that seemed part of the table. Hedwig, who had worked thirteen years for Frau Furstenburg, was a dear, typically German hausfrau with salt-and-pepper hair parted in the middle and done in braids wrapped around her head. Since I spoke some German, I soon became one of her favorites. Her twinkly eyes and wry sense of humor belied her appearance. My friend Andy, who was almost part of the family for a time, used to love to pull Hedwig's leg; he'd call her "Heddy," and add, "Do you know that this is the name of one of our most glamorous movie stars in the States?" She would blush, cover her face with her apron, and rush into the kitchen. She was a good cook; she tried to make things we liked and generally succeeded—except the time she stewed precious tomatoes, as Germans do I guess, instead of using them for a fresh salad.

I found I was to be in charge of three clubs. In addition to this big one for enlisted men in the theater building, there was a smaller officers' club nearby, and a third was shortly to open at the Winterland Ice Stadium, built for the 1936 Winter Olympics. The stadium was quite a layout with three rinks. A large ice area with VIP seats centered on one side was used for hockey games twice a week and for ice shows on Wednesdays and weekends, when they had lovely colored designs frozen in the ice. Music to skate to was played all day long at a smaller rink for practice and recreation. The club was in a suite of rooms above, with windows overlooking the ice. They may have been press boxes at one time but had been newly decorated for us. It was really swish—all shiny and new, with special composition floors that wouldn't dull skates.

Once I'd settled in, I wrote home about my work.

Garmisch Partenkirchen, Bavaria, Monday night, January 28, 1946

It's good to be actually running a club of my own again, or should I say three? We have a German manager at each one; they do most of the detail work and handle a staff of ninety-some Germans.

Garmisch has three military outfits, which is confusing at first—administratively I mean. The war is over, and the guys who come from all over the European Theater are on furlough or leave. To run this center there's a battalion of the 47th Infantry, a 35th Field Artillery Group, and the military Winter Sports Center which handles programming; so I have three different groups to get stuff from! I find I'm taking over a well-run operation, and all I have to do is just try to improve it. That should be fun.

Pete comes from Munich each weekend, and we are together as much as my schedule allows. His mother trained him well, for each week he writes his bread-and-butter letter, saying how much coming out to our house means to him; it's like a "home away from home." Pete takes advantage of his tour of duty to come to Garmisch, where the men can use skis or skates free of charge and enjoy one of the swankiest resort towns in Germany, in contrast to many who hang around the Red Cross club and moan that "the bars don't even open till four o'clock."

๛

Our officers' club was in a small storefront building that had belonged to the Krenners. They were friends of Richard Strauss, Jr., and his wife and complained to them about the apartment they'd been moved to. Frau Strauss was a pert little redhead. Their house was not far from ours, and several times she rode over on her bicycle. I'd invite her in for coffee but reluctantly refuse her invitations to reciprocate, for I didn't want to be under any kind of obligation should she try to wangle special favors for their friends the Krenners. Over coffee she told us about their home in Vienna, which at one time during the war had housed fifty Russians and fifty dogs. It was now an American officers' mess with a huge bar in the dining room and "more bottles than I've ever seen in my whole life!" she said.

A triumvirate of doctors from the hospital in Munich were often at our officers' club. We invited them out to the house, and went skiing with them. There were two Eds. Ed One was a Yalie. Ed Two, from Harvard, was a descendant of a historic European family. Rafe, a doctor from Georgia, became my special friend and date—except on the ski slopes: he and Ed One were great skiers, so there I teamed up with Ed Two, who was more my speed. On our first day out, the four of us did about three runs of the Kochelburg, the chairlift run nearest town. Then, after lunch, we rode the cable car to the Kreutzek and came down the Olympic Trail. I took a couple of great spills but got down in one piece, and after that no slope intimidated me! It didn't boost my pride that day, though, to watch the success of several skiers who had lost a leg.

We have a way of forgetting what the war did to just ordinary people. The Germans, great brew lovers, made do with beer that had hardly any alcohol content. It must have tasted like dishwater to them. I'm not sure how rationing worked; but things you can get hooked on, like tobacco and coffee seemed unavailable. That's why we could use our cigarettes for legal tender, and at the club we saved our coffee grounds for the hospitals and rest homes. I still have a two-foot-square coffee table with a tile top—the tiles handpainted with *alpenblumen* and insignia of the U.S. military groups who were stationed in Garmisch—which was brought by a little black-habited nun to say "thank you." She'd come weekly to pick up coffee grounds, pulling her sled with a box attached for her precious cargo.

We ran tours for the GIs, using army trucks, to see Linderhof Castle and Ettal Monastery of the Benedictine monks (known for their famous liqueur), and also to Oberammergau so the guys could see where the famed Passion Play was produced each ten years. Miniature Linderhof was a gem, with its Dresden china figurines, crystal chandeliers, gold threaded tapestries and such. It was built by Ludwig, the Mad King of Bavaria, who had a castle complex. Herrenchiemsee was his attempt to copy Louis XIV's Palace of Versailles; many-turreted Neuschwanstein was perched atop its very own mountain.

Garmisch, Bavaria, Germany, March 14, 1946
We've really worked hard making changes I wanted around the club. We no longer have just coffee and donuts. Herr Roland, is a master conditor, what we'd call a pastry cook. That's the way they learn trades over here, by start-

ing as apprentice and moving on up through journeyman, etc., until one is a "master." Herr Roland was not just a master but a magician. What he could do with that donut mix was a miracle, but when I had talked Red Cross out of some white flour, things really started happening.

We got not only white flour but also eggs—not powdered eggs (which the Army often cooks in huge square pans and cuts in inch-thick squares that are often green on the bottom if you turn them over) but eggs in the shell! Granted they've been preserved in something like the old-fashioned waterglass and taste a bit musty, but they still top powdered ones. Once we started serving eggs on morning shifts, I got the idea of accompanying them with cinnamon rolls.

Herr Roland also makes cakes and cookies, often with lovely icing he concocts out of the powdered milk and donut mix we get from Red Cross. We did have to use another kind of "mix" replacing the fresh milk and ice cream for our soda fountains; but you couldn't tell the difference. Our milk shakes and malts are so thick you have to eat them with a spoon. We have sodas too, and hamburgers "with." Some guys order about five hamburgers and a malt, line them up, and dig in with a big grin on their face. Munching away they say things like, "This is more like home than anything I've run into over here!"

Just had a contest to name the club, and we had over four hundred entries from guys all over Europe. We had radio publicity on AFN-Munich and offered a Swiss watch to the winner. So now it's the Olympic Club, and today I got plywood to make a beautiful sign for the front—huge letters on a background of the colorful intertwined Olympic circles. We have a doorman in Bavarian garb—*lederhosen*, green felt hat with band and brush. Behind him are two signs we had to put up.

Z I V I L I S T E N
EINTRITT VERBOTEN
U S ARMY PROPERTY

THIS CLUB IS FOR AMERICAN
MILITARY & CIVILIAN PERSONNEL
ALLIED MILITARY IN UNIFORM WILL BE
ADMITTED AS GUESTS OF AMERICANS
ANYONE IN CIVILIAN CLOTHES WILL PLEASE
SHOW IDENTIFICATION

We completely redecorated the main part of the club. It has beautiful hardwood floors, but the black rubber soles on GI boots had made the finish pretty grimy. So Tony Seethaler, our German manager, said that if I could requisition some candles from Red Cross, he could mix the wax with vinegar to make floor wax. He had the staff steel-wool off all the black stuff and apply this wax, and you should see the floors now! They're beautiful, and Tony has the help keeping them that way.

The walls are now a soft rose, and a local artist painted colorful Bavarian scenes on panels between pillars. Artists and craftsmen here can make wonderful things. I have silver jewelry made from U.S. coins, and a great leather camera case for my Kodak Retina cost $15 in the PX.

Things have quieted down after all the ski meets, ice hockey tournaments, and such. We got to know some of the topnotch sportsmen from our theater, plus the Italian theater, and it's hard to see them go. There was Carl Bohler, the champion ski jumper of the ETO, who was afraid to fly in planes! There was the hockey team for the 78th Division in Berlin, who were sent down to Garmisch to play hockey; it was "duty" for them! They had their own house, housekeeper, and cook.

We've had culture too! A week ago Thursday the Munich Symphony played in our theater and we had a party afterward at the house. We invited Kurt Leimers, the concert pianist who comes to play for us now and then; Dean Mahin, editor of the *Winterland* (our newspaper); Gerhard Hauptman's son, one of Germany's leading poet-philosophers; our neighbors, Mr. and Mrs. Richard Strauss, Jr.; and handsome, twenty-one-year-old Harry Brown, who was

conducting at the age of thirteen and had just guest-con-
ducted for the Chicago and Philadelphia symphony
orchestras.

It was a good evening. Kurt Leimers played, as we
sipped cognac—a special treat for the Germans. They loved
the food too. Strauss and Hauptman wore tight knee-
breeches and flat dancing pumps with bows, which empha-
sized Richard's amazing height of six-four or more. He
spoke only broken English. I felt dwarfed as Dean and I
were trying to explain to him what "snow job" meant. At
one point, he crooked his head and said to me, "Miss
Kochendoerfer, I think you must have the classic American
profile." I thought a minute. Then it dawned on me it was
the 'Indian profile.' To him the 'Indian' was classic American! He again was insistent that we tell them when we
could come to their home, where their father had composed
some of his music. He's in Switzerland just now.

ᠷ

Another letter started off thanking Mom for "the surprise of
my life, a pair of nylons!" The other gals had all received
some, and I must have complained, but I told them not to
worry about my "sock" situation: "I can always wear the rayon ones from the PX, even though they aren't very glamorous." Nylons were hard to get anywhere, even in the
States. Stories are legion of what a GI could get from British,
French, or German women for a pair of nylons.

One aspect of the somewhat artificial life we led was that
some Red Cross girls and WACs expected to return to the
States to marry a military man who'd sworn he would di-
vorce his wife. I'm sure many men actually believed while
they were over there that they *would* desert their wives and
families. Coming home for some family men might be difficult, after the "single" freedom they'd experienced in the
ETO. For others, I'm sure the war years would soon seem
but a dream.

I told my family that I would start sending home some
things—no longer "loot" but what I'd acquired with our occu-

pation marks—or, more often, in black market deals for cigarettes. The Germans preferred cigarettes to money. I suppose
some did smoke them, but others used them like cash. They
would pay 50 marks ($5.00) for three packs of cigarettes that
cost us seven cents a pack—and these prices were mild compared with what they were in Berlin. Kids got into the act too;
if you smoked at outdoor activities, there would be two or
three German kids eagerly watching, ready to pounce the
minute you threw down a butt. And realizing what it meant
for them I wondered more than once how many more puffs to
take. They sold the butts they collected to firms who made re-
constituted cigs. I tried those one time—that was enough!

Garmisch, Germany, April 22, 1946

I'm terribly busy on the job (believe it or not) what with
all the changes in personnel, closing the Olympic Ice Stadium club, and getting the other two converted to their summer settings. I don't know what I'd do without Tony; if I
ever ask for anything, I know it will be done when I want it
done and in the best possible way. A former leading busi-
nessman, he seems to know all the angles of getting stuff
that's difficult and sometimes seemingly impossible to get.
And at the house we now have Herr Koch to lay fires and
shovel snow and Frace von Stern to help Hedwig.

Last week was Easter Sunday. I left the States just two
years ago, on April 8, 1944! It's a big celebration over here—
almost like Christmas. Good Friday morning at breakfast,
Frau von Stern and her daughter had decorated our table
with little bunny cookies and precious almond fudge, pretty
napkins, and nosegays of flowers at each plate.

There was a sunrise service scheduled outdoors at the
Kreutzekhaus, and two early cable cars to take folks up.
Each car holds twenty-six persons standing up; skis are
usually clamped on top. Since they were to go terribly early and Rafe didn't bring me home until late, I talked him
into sleeping on a sofa in the living room instead of going
back to the hotel.

I was supposed to get everyone up but overslept. We had to rush into clothes, jump into the jeep, and race to the cable car station. We made the last run. I wish you could see this country when the sky is azure blue, the craggy snow-capped peaks and green mountain sides springing out in all sorts of color with early *alpenblumen*. I'm getting a painting of the beautiful Alpspitz—my favorite mountain.

As our car emptied at the top and we joined those already there, we found to our dismay that it was the minister whose alarm hadn't gone off. As we waited, we gathered around the little cross they always have at the tops of mountains here in Bavaria. You know how silently exciting and impressive sunrises are anyway. So try to picture one on a mountain top, with the surrounding higher peaks around in shadow, as the rays shoot between them, setting the whole eastern sky ablaze. We held our breath in a deep realization that some of the most profound experiences in life occur in silence.

We had a parade of handmade Easter bonnets at the club Saturday night. We'd gotten together a big pile of stuff that the guys could use, and I wish you could have seen some of their creations. Lili Daché could have commissioned a couple of them! The winner, who got a Swiss watch, wore a lovely little model of blue, perked down over one eye, with real yellow flowers edging the brim and the band that held it on, and a hamburger "with" plunked in the center of the top.

This reminds me of a handsome blue-eyed blond who was often in the club. When we started having the great new menu I asked him whether he didn't think it was super. He said, "Yes, Vi, but . . ." "But what? What else could you want?" "Well, Vi, how's about a blonde on toast?" So I cut out a pic from a girlie magazine I got from some of the guys—a breezy unclad blonde, leaning back with legs up. I mounted it on cardboard with a little standard behind, put her on a piece of toast and served it to him the next time he was in.

It was a time of transition once again. Joan and Frenchie were leaving at the beginning of May, but Mary from South Bend, Indiana, joined us, and a week earlier two had come from the Clubmobile Department—Elsie, a blonde Norwegian type, taller than I (which I liked), and her friend Martina, strikingly different, with long glossy black hair and bright blue eyes. She'd been a New York model.

Garmisch, Germany, June 18, 1946

Did I tell you that we now have a tailor shop, where guys can have alterations and pressing done while they wait? German women come in to do mending and sewing too. We're opening a craft shop; we have Mackay Radio cable service to the States now; and in another week we'll have our direct wire to Nuremberg and our own teletype with operator. Artist Harry does great sketches of the guys (his German name is Kurt, but he thinks Harry is more American!). We also have a woman who cuts silhouettes, a complete information and interpretive service, and package wrapping, plus the great chow. And the hallway walls are filled with notices of THINGS TO DO IN GARMISCH.

Because we can't allow GIs to bring frauleins into the clubs, I've been choosy in hiring cute waitresses; which reminds me that Karl, the typically handsome, blonde, blue-eyed German who's a professional ski instructor, has asked me to go places with him. But though it's OK for the military men to date British and French girls or German frauleins, it's considered unacceptable for us to date a German man. I wonder who's protecting whom!

◆

My next letter home was about a trip to Venice. It all happened because one day Lyn came to me with the news that her special friend was leaving for home and wanted her to go off on a trip before he left. I realized that if I let her go, others would feel they should have the same privilege. So I called a meeting of our RC staff and suggested that if each of us was willing to cover by taking extra schedules, one by one we could each have an unofficial short leave. The gals loved the idea. When it was my turn, I went to Venice with Rafe and another doctor from Munich. Our Danielle Hotel was right on the Grand Canal. We bargained for moonlight gondola rides with cigarettes (one price for Luckies and Camels, more for Old Golds) and lucked out with a singing gondolier. I bought a new two-piece swim suit at a shop on St. Mark's Square, and we had a heavenly day swimming at the Lido, returning from Venice through Cortina where the MTO/ETO ski meets were held. I found no one at headquarters had missed me, so all was well.

When I first got to Garmisch, we had had two jeeps. Later, Dewey (one of the GIs assigned to us) had insisted that since he was going home, I should take a jeep he'd had "off the record" since France. That's how we got "Nix Chocolat." Later, with gas rationed and vehicle use tightened up, I was standing outside the Post Hotel one Sunday with Rafe and his friend Robbie when their commanding officer in Munich happened to see us and walked over. Looking at the bumper markings on the guys' vehicle, he said, "Captain Robinson, isn't that one of our jeeps?" "No, sir," Robbie answered, and turning, he put the key in my hand. "It's been transferred." I'm not sure just how he got away with it, but that's how we got "Lucille." (I mentioned a key; we needed a key not to start a jeep but to lock the steering wheel with chain and padlock.)

Not much later a directive came down that we had to register all our army vehicles, and there I sat with two illegal jeeps! What to do? First we parked them behind the house in a lovely patio area, but people would ask why. We thought of driving them up some mountain road and abandoning them but gave up that idea too. Finally I went to the sergeant at the motor pool and told him my dilemma. He said, "Well, Vi, if you'll bring them over next Thursday when we're not busy, we can dismantle them and save the parts to use on your other two!" And that's what we did. Seems as senior club director, I was to be constantly involved in vehicle deals!

There was a letter from Pete dated June 17, 1946, telling that five days after he landed in the United States he was a full-fledged civilian.

Strikes, shortages, costs—no matter what—the States are absolutely wonderful. I must admit that I was a bit dubiuos about this country, but when we landed and took those buses to Camp Kilmer, and saw all the cars, people all dressed up, buildings in one piece, and PX's just jammed with things that were unheard of in the ET, I quickly regained my courage.

Clothing is very hard to get and very expensive. I'm really lucky since most of my old clothes still fit! Shirts are hard to get and quite expensive. Manhattan shirts that used to be $2.25 are now five dollars. We're really having a period of inflation, but I don't think it will last too long. The labor situation is looking better and as soon as production increases, more competition will return, and prices will go down, we hope. But no matter what happens, we won't starve and we'll always be a hell of a lot better off than the people on the other side.

Shortly after the trip to Venice I was in Munich on ARC business and stayed over at the 24th General Dispensary, where Rafe and Mac were on the medical staff. When Rafe suggested I stay with the Red Cross girls who were assigned there, I met Claire, who was going on leave to Rome the same week I had leave scheduled to the Riviera, both on conducted tours. I mentioned that I'd love to drive to Nice if I had someone to go with me. That was all Claire needed. She said she'd forget Rome and go with me.

This time we had orders written on stationery of the 24th General Dispensary, and Rafe had pulled strings to get the twenty jerry cans of gas we took along. He first tried to talk us out of this as too dangerous; but when we wouldn't listen he insisted that we take the gas in the trailer. We cleared Brenner Pass, heaving sighs of relief as the officer stamped our questionable orders and made them legal.

I could write a small volume describing the trip, with jeep trouble again, flat tires, skidding off the road because of the trailer, the excitement of crossing more Italian mountains, and the border crossing at Monte Carlo, which cost us only a flashlight that the French border guard admired.

Our days were spent with Air Force chaps whom we met while promenading on the boardwalk at Nice. My date was always Andy for sunning, swimming, biking, exploring expeditions, and nightclubbing. He was delightful, much younger than I but with an adventurous spirit that attracted us to each other. Andy had divorced his wife for infidelity and said he was off women. I countered, "Of course, Andy, till the next one comes along" He was stationed in Marseille, and after I got home and sent him copies of pictures I'd taken, the letters started flowing, suggesting I was that next one. Once again I spoke of our age difference, but that didn't deter Andy. After one try at a transfer that put him in Paris, he finally swung another that brought him to Munich. There he spent nearly every weekend in Garmisch and became one of our family.

My letter home about the Nice trip again wallowed in superlatives, but those were the words we used as we went to places we never dreamed we'd see. I knew that much of what I thought picuresque was made attractive by its primitive nature and the poverty it reflected. Even so, I wondered whether those peasants cutting whole grain in fields with hand scythes might not be more happy and content than many Americans. That was their way of life, and they accepted it without question.

15 Trails, Trials, and High Finance

When I got back from Nice, things had been happening at the club. For one, a new replacement had come in. But the devastating news came from Elsie, who told me Tony had been in jail for nearly a week. I couldn't believe it, but Elsie went on to say, "MPs burst into the Seethaler's home, found several cartons of cigarettes and $136 in American money," which was illegal for him to have. Frau Seethaler and the club staff had been wonderful in taking over but were eagerly waiting till I got back: "When Miss Vi comes, she will fix everything." There was little I could do, however, for we'd had a directive that if any members of our indigenous staff were removed, we were not to question it.

I went to see Tony and when he came into the room, my heart sank. Instead of the cocky, chubby little man we all knew and loved, he looked deflated and really ill. He couldn't talk for a few minutes. His mouth quivered so that I thought he was going to cry, but finally he told me the story. It seems that a waitress Tony had fired squealed to her MP boyfriend. The raid came that same night. Tony said he was keeping the cigarettes for Dewey, one of the GIs who worked for us. But he'd been selling wine for diamonds and jewelry and American currency to GIs as far back as the 10th Armoured. As one of the leading businessmen in Garmisch, Tony's pride was crushed. He begged me to try to get him out on bail.

I went to talk with the American officer in charge of indigenous personnel for the Military Government to say that we couldn't run the club without him. I was told, as part of a long ranting lecture, that Tony "had had it and would have a hard time explaining the money." The way he said it got my dander up, and I retorted, "Captain B., we all know some of the really rotten things that go on in Garmisch and you don't do a thing." He ignored that and went on ranting about the Germans who sell cigarettes who were the downfall of the whole system. I countered, "Captain B. both you and I know that we Americans black-market all over the place, and nothing's done about that."

When Rafe learned of this, he cussed (something Rafe never did) and told about some shady deals this very officer himself was involved in. Tony was sentenced anyway. Because of his health they put him on an outside detail working in the woods, and maybe that was a lifesaver for him. But it was hard on us, and on him too in other ways.

One night at midnight the radio program was interrupted by an official voice: "As of now your money is no good. You will report to the executive finance officer at the Marketplatz tomorrow and report what you have." This was the military trying to control the black market. Many were making thousands to send home.

They'd tried once before by issuing each of us a little account book. Our earnings were entered on the left, and on the right any money orders we'd sent to the States. Of course this was to be heavier on the earning side, for supposedly we'd spent something. But because the guys complained— "I won that in a poker game!" and so on—regulations were loosened to allow us to send home amounts up to 110 percent of our earnings.

But human ingenuity and greed will not be deterred by rules, and some didn't just send their money home. I mentioned the hockey team from 78th in Berlin who spent the season in Garmisch playing hockey 'on duty.' One of the players would get regular furloughs back to Berlin to see how his night club was doing—the club he'd bought with his black market earnings! Another ploy: sometimes you could find someone who wasn't sending home his or her entire paycheck, and pay that person a premium to include your extra.

Next day I stood in the money line chatting with friends. "How much are you going to declare?" We all had more than we'd earned. The unforgettable part was played by a GI two ahead of me in line. The colonel checking this chap's book looked up and said, "Hey, Buddy, you're taking a loss!" The GI answered, "No I'm not, sir. I spent that money!"

If all this sounds like high finance, I should report that I made $250 a month after a second raise—which I'd had to ask for. When I heard that one RC gal who was always flubbing up and being called into headquarters had gotten a raise, I sent off a letter to Wiesbaden to the effect that if we ran a good show and didn't cause them any trouble, they'd easily forget all about us. First I got a raise for Elsie, who hadn't ever had one, and then said that I felt I should have one too! I accompanied that request with a recommendation from Ellie, which did it: "Miss Kochendoerfer is an outstanding Club Director in all respects. She has a well-trained staff, does a fine administrative job, has unique program ideas which display a fine sense of timing and coordination, and has an excellent relationship with the Military. It is therefore recommended that Miss Kochendoerfer be given a change of classification and a salary increase."

In a letter home on July 15, I noted that even though we did work long and hard, I'd often write just about leaves, days off, skiing, and dates, and that we always seemed to be having a drink. Actually, this was a good part of the show for everyone, especially the guys who had little to do. Unfortunately some GIs would drink anything that gave them a high, things like antifreeze in what was called "buzz bomb juice," and sometimes they'd end up in the hospital blind or critically ill, or even in the morgue. What we offered guests at our house was not so lethal, however. We'd got a monthly liquor ration and would send Elsie to pick it up, because the GI in charge liked her and usually threw in a couple of extra bottles of something.

Meanwhile, back at the club, our German artist, Harry, and our new girl, Darcy, were a great combination. Big attractions were their painted life-size characters with faces cut out so that GIs could supply their own face and have their pictures taken. There was a ski jumper leaning way forward, a Bavarian chap in lederhosen and green felt hat and all. There was a bicycle built for two, and a "man of distinction"— a well-dressed chap lounging in a robe on an overstuffed chair with a pedigreed dog at this side. For St. Patrick's Day, Darcy devised a "kissing the Blarney Stone" scene.

Harry's artwork was also on the signs labeling the various services we offered the GIs. Elsie and I had sat up half a night with a bottle of Scotch dreaming up the names for the "Clip Joint" barber shop, the "Drape Shape" tailor shop, the "Tell Schnell" cable service, "Pack your Wraps, Wrap your Packs," and "Nails on the House," where Josephine Schneider held forth. She was a favorite with the guys, for she spoke good English and could hold her own in their GI give and take.

At one point I was getting compliments from the club staff which I didn't quite understand at first. Word had gotten around town, I found out, that on Friday night at the weekly 30, 60 and 90 meter Olympic ski jumps, word had come over the loud speaker: "Miss Kochendoerfer is the Champion American Woman Skier!" Someone had learned it seems, that I'd won a little gold ski in a time race on the Horn Trail. Although I wasn't a racer, friends talked me into doing the time runs on the steep, tricky Horn Trail. It was icy that day, which made it even faster; and in side-slipping down a long slope near the finish, I hit ruts and spread-eagled toward the finish line. Spectators yelled, "Crawl it, Vi!" I did, on all fours, and made it in the three minutes which qualified for the gold ski. This really didn't mean a thing, since none of us were all that great, but I wore that gold ski on my ski cap for years.

In November 1945 the war crimes trials began in Nuremberg, and I was able to attend one day of the proceedings. I had earlier driven through Nurenberg on my way to Bayreuth, where Mom had wanted me to visit some distant cousins. Cousin Ernst took me to see the huge Festspielhaus in Bayreuth which Richard Wagner had designed when he moved there in 1872, and where his wife continued the Bay-

reuth Festivals after his death. Ernst said Hitler gave speeches
many times from a special box on an outside balcony. Wagner's home was now an officers' club.

It was Rafe who had some connections that got us into the
trials in the fall of 1946. We arrived in Nuremberg early
enough to drive around the city, stopping at the huge stadium where we've all seen pictures of Hitler giving his mes-
merizing speeches. Old Town, surrounded by ancient walls,
had provided a beautiful target and been pretty much leveled. Receiving programs for the "International Military Tri-
bunal, Nuremberg, Germany, 1945-46," we entered the court
where "drapes and carpets imported from France hushed
the crowded room" in which this "unprecedented test of international morality" was taking place. The indictment read:

The United States of America, the French Republic, the United
Kingdom of Great Britain and Northern Ireland, and the Union of
Soviet Socialist Republics against Herman Wilhelm Göring, Rudolf
Hess, Joachim von Ribbentrop, Robert Ley, Wilhelm Keitel, Ernst
Kaltenbrunner, Alfred Rosenberg, Hans Frank, Wilhelm Frick, Ju-
lius Streicher, Walter Funk, Hjalmar Schact, Gustav Krupp von Boh-
len und Halback, Karl Donitz, Erich Raeder, Baldur von Schirach,
Fritz Sauckel, Alfred Jodl, Martin Bormann, Franz von Papen, Ar-
thur Seiss-Inquart, Albert Speer, Constantin von Neurath, and
Hans Fritzsche, individually and as members of any of the following groups of organizations to which they respectively belonged,
namely Die Reichsregierung (Reich cabinet); Das Korps der Poli-
tischen Leiter der Nationalsozialistischen Deutschen Arbeiterpartei
[leadership corps of the Nazi party]; Die Schutzstaffeln der Nation-
alsocialistischen Deutschen Arbeiterpartei [commonly the SS] and
including Die Sturmabteilungen der N.S.D.A.P. [the SA] and the
General Staff and High Command of the German Armed Forces.

Long indictments were described under Count One—The
Common Plan or Conspiracy; Count Two—Crimes against
Peace; Count Three—War Crimes; and Count Four—Crimes
against Humanity.

It was the first time I'd experienced the use of earphones
that could be dialed for English, French, German, or Rus-

sian. And I was entranced when all twenty-one of the defendants (three of those listed did not stand trial) marched in under guard—led by Goering, a tall, pudgy bulk of a man—and seated in two rows along the left-hand side of the courtroom, with Goering in the front most visible seat. Included in the program was a numbered diagram of the seating, keyed to names to show who sat where; evidently, all defendants had to sit through all the sessions. The day we were there, Field Marshall Keitel (whose luxurious headquarters we'd seen in Berchtesgaden) was on trial. The program said of him that between 1938 and 1945 he was

Chief of the High Command of the German Armed Forces, member of the Secret Cabinet Council, member of the Council of Ministers for the Defense of the Reich, and Field Marshal. The defendant *Keitel* used the foregoing positions, his personal influence and his intimate connection with the Fuhrer in such a manner that: he promoted the military preparations for war set forth in Count One; he participated in the political planning and preparation of the Nazi conspirators for Wars of Aggression and Wars in Violation of International Treaties, Agreements and Assurances set forth in Counts One and Two; he authorized, directed and participated in the War Crimes set forth in Counts Three and Four, including particularly the War Crimes and Crimes against Humanity involved in the ill treatment of prisoners of war and of the civilian population of occupied territories.

For each defendant there was a lengthy statement like this. The "Statement of Individual Responsibility" for Goering set forth an even longer list of positions (including "Successor Designate to Hitler)" and litany of offenses on all four counts (including, under Count Four, "a wide variety of crimes against persons and property." That day reminded us unforgettably of why we were over there. We left, wondering how the trials would all come out.

In addition to Rafe and the other men in my life on the Garmisch scene, there were three professional Bavarian ski instructors who would ski with me if I went to the Kreutzek without a date. Tony Woerndle broke his leg shortly after I arrived, and we visited him in the hospital. I met him again many years later at a party in Aspen, Colorado. The youngest of the three was Karl Feit, another of those strikingly handsome Aryan blue-eyed blonds with wavy hair. I often skied the whole day with Karl when he could get the time off. He helped me build up my leg strength so I could attempt the Olympic trail the whole way down without stopping, and one day I finally did it. I was ecstatic, even though at the bottom my legs just collapsed like sponge rubber.

The Bavarian I spent the most time skiing with was Willie Schaeffler, a rather stocky man who used to take me off the trail into deep snow; and when I'd cry out, "But Willy, I can't do this," he'd retort, "Miss Vi, if you're going to ski you have to learn how to ski in all kinds of snow." He said he'd have to get an American girlfriend to improve his English. When I told him that we'd often kid at the house and say, "Some evening we'd like to shock the military by appearing with a German date," Willie said eagerly, "Miss Vi, you just let me know when, and I'll put on my best suit." But this was still *verboten* for us. Later, Willy married the daughter of an American officer, came to the States, and coached Denver University's ski team (I heard it was the first time Dartmouth had been beaten). He also laid out trails for the Winter Olympics at Squaw Valley, California, in 1960, and he was so noted for his style of skiing—called *Wedeln*—that he appeared on the cover of *Ski Illustrated*.

16 Leaving Garmisch the Hard Way

It was sometime in November 1946 that a woman in the uniform of the German Red Cross was ushered into my office at the club. She said, "I come to you with a big problem I do hope you can help me with. You perhaps don't know, but there are thousands of German refugee children who were separated from their families and moved into barracks buildings at different places for the duration. We want so much to have a Christmas celebration for them."

Since we were to get what seemed to be half a truckload of candy, gum, and other goodies from headquarters, I agreed that we would help if they could bring the children to us. She asked, "How many can you have?" Since the civic theater in our building seated twelve hundred, I told her if she'd take the responsibility of getting them there, we'd take care of twelve hundred!

We had a staff of seventy-some Germans at that club, so I put them to work when they weren't busy elsewhere, first helping make 1,200 gifts and then wrapping 2,400 parcels. We had candy, gum and stuff from Red Cross and we could get nuts and fruit from the commissary. Presents we had to scrounge or make; there was no place to buy them! We used some of the things Red Cross had sent for the men—toothbrushes and toothpaste, combs, and so on; we made little notebooks (paper was precious to the Germans); the tailor shop stitched little ducks and animals for beanbags and we filled them with beans from the commissary.

Then someone suggested enlisting the help of the German generals at the internment camp where 450 were awaiting the outcome of the Nuremberg trials. I went out to the camp at the edge of town and asked for the commandant. I felt as if I were in the movies as this tall lean officer walked in in high black leather boots, long black leather coat and all. He spoke enough English to understand what I wanted and to tell me that they did have a craft shop. If I could bring the materials, he'd have the men make things for us.

We gathered everything we could think of—cloth, cardboard, tin cans, glue, paint, wire, string. We also made suggestions, such as providing patterns for cutting ducks from plywood, which could be painted and mounted on rectangles of wood, using checkers we brought for wheels, to make pull toys. When I went out to take more materials and see how they were doing, the movie atmosphere continued: as we walked through the shop, the men came to attention and clicked heels for the major.

It was fascinating to see pompous general types making tiny things for children, and I couldn't believe the craftsmanship. There were whole villages of little painted Bavarian chalets, complete with tiny rocks on the roofs. There were room furnishings such as miniature upholstered sofas, bookcases, with tiny books that could be removed. I loved it all but was somewhat dismayed, for we needed quantity more than quality. I tried to explain this to the major; reminding him of the patterns, I asked in my broken German, "Varrum keine ducks?" (my version of "Why no ducks?"). He found the patterns on a shelf and said something to the effect of "They are so primitive."

Nevertheless, we finally collected enough and finished the job of wrapping with the help of some army wives, who had been arriving, labeling the presents by age and "boy" or "girl." The Garmisch Little Theater had promised to present a play in German, and we were to have St. Nicholas there. When word got out as to what we were doing, Radio Munich people called to ask whether they could broadcast the party. I was thrilled. And during all of this I'd think of our kids' party in England and compare the two.

The Monday of Christmas week we helped with another party for the German children of Garmisch, given in our theater by the GIs and the German Youth Program, and that evening in the club a program was presented by a group of refugee (mostly Polish) children. The guys loved their performance and feeding the kids afterwards.

On the day of the big party it was snowing. I can still see the sleighs pulling up to the club with the big curved runners up front and the seats crowded with tiny tots who had been brought into Garmisch by train from Mittenwald on the Austrian border, from Oberammergau seventeen kilometers away, and other little towns.

Now please try to imagine twelve hundred kids being ushered into our warm building from out in the cold, each bundled in coat and mittens and scarf to be taken off and stashed. Then the donuts and hot chocolate we had for them seemed to play tricks with their bladders. I'm not sure how many hundreds had to go to the toilet, but we had GIs acting as ushers to take the kids to the restrooms in shifts.

We fed them first, and then the program began. Since these were German kids, Harry, as St. Nicholas in his white robes and tall miter was master of ceremonies. He talked to the excited children and introduced a play titled *The Christmas Star*, about a little lame girl to whom miraculous things happened on a Christmas Eve. Radio Munich was there, and because it was a joint effort of the Deutsches Rote Kreutz (German Red Cross) and us, the mayor of Munich came too. He interviewed me, going on about how good we were to help, and then spoke to the children. Next came Christmas carols, and I sat there with a big lump in my throat and tears streaming down my cheeks. At home on Christmas Eve, we'd always gone to church for the program of St. Martins Lutheran Parochial School, which was done in German, so from childhood I'd known the many carols that came from Germany—"Schtille Nacht, Heilege Nacht," "O Du Froeliche," and others. The kids knew them all, and if you can imagine twelve hundred tiny voices making a big sound of happiness, you can get some idea of what it all meant.

The only way we could think of to distribute the gifts was to give them to the children on the way out. As they came from the auditorium into the lobby, they got the gift of candy and fruit, and then near the other doors the gift of toys. We need not have been concerned about being mobbed, for these German children seemed well brought up. They all said their *danke shoens*, and some girls even did a little curtsey. A couple of the boys clicked their heels! The one I shall not forget was a tiny girl with long blonde curls and big blue eyes. As I gave her the second package she looked up, eyes wide, and said, "Ich habe eins!" (I have one!) She just couldn't believe she was getting more than one gift. Andy, who was helping us, said, "Vi, this is one Christmas I'll never forget." I agreed.

Later I received several thank-you letters, one of which I've kept.

To the American Red Cross
Garmisch-Partenkirchen

As the father of one of the children which were your guests last Saturday afternoon, I thank you for what you gave them, how you gave and that you did. So soon after the war, the peace treaty not yet being signed, we take this initiative as a sign of good will for reconciliation and mutual understanding.

After years of hatred and destruction, these children are longing for love and peace and will understand your intention. We adults thank you for this Christmas joy of our children, we thank you for all you did for our youth generally, for our refugees, we thank you for all your statesmen do and did to reconstruct a new and happier Germany, a better Europe and a world worthy to live in.
(It was signed "Dr. G. Dufey.")

The night after the party was Christmas Eve. We had a special program for the guys at the club, and at ten we all left on sleighs to go caroling around Garmisch, coming back after eleven for something to eat before midnight services in our theater. Christmas Day we served a special breakfast for the men, went to church with those who wanted to, and later had a party for them at which we handed out cigarettes and candy and gifts of sweaters and scarfs sent from the States.

It was another month before I found time to write home. The bright spot of that month was getting Tony back!

Garmisch, Germany, Janaury 19, 1947

I realize that every time I write (and remember there are long lapses between times) it's usually after I've been some place or something special has happened that I feel I should tell you all about. Or, if not, we're bound to relate the high spots from the past month or so, till it must sound as though we've done nothing more than entertain ourselves.

But truly, I've never worked harder than I have over here, and I believe more so in Garmisch than anywhere else. If one thinks of being responsible for supervising a staff of seventy-five (hiring, firing, schedules, etc.) and a snack bar that takes in $6,000 to $8,000 a month (ordering supplies, planning and printing menus), with electricity off from four to seven each day and our ovens, coffee makers and ice cream freezers, air compressers, etc., all electric, so you have to bake at night, etc., plus running a tailor shop, barber shop, shoe-shine, manicure, voice recording, checkrooms, and dealing with hundreds of information requests, planning tours plus a program for every evening and many afternoons, filing weekly, monthly, and special reports for the Red Cross and the Army, keeping GIs and civilians happy each day and entertaining them, talking with, taking care of their million and one requests that they can't find answers for anywhere else—they think we can do anything!

All that, plus keeping the ARC gals happy and running our own household, keeping two vehicles on the road when there are often no parts, gas shortages, etc., there's never a dull moment, never two days alike, and hardly a night when I go to bed and don't think of something I forgot to do, or write a list of stuff to do the next day. Like just yesterday we had to fire a man on the staff when Toni discovered he'd been with the SS. He seemed such a nice chap it was hard to believe; but I guess the tattoo gave him away one day; and as I said, we're not supposed to ask questions.

I had some personal publicity too. A picture was published showing me with a German driver of their famous three-wheeled trucks as he delivered some furniture to the club. The one I liked best was a photo of me with Jimmie Worback and his dog Blackie. Jimmie was about twelve, a cute kid in a miniature 82d Airborne uniform complete with jump boots and jump wings. He'd been a mascot of 82d up in Berlin, and I'm not sure just how he got to Garmisch—but he did, with his faithful Blackie. We were so happy to see each other again.

We're trying to make contact with his relatives in America. Jimmie told us he'd been born in Brooklyn and had gone to Sicily in 1939 with his German-born mother. After she was killed, he wandered over Europe as a GI mascot and found a permanent berth with the 82d. He was as lovable as his dog Blackie was trained. He'd bring Blackie to my office, have him lie down under a bench and say, "Stay there, Blackie." And Blackie would, till Jimmie got back, often hours later. Our picture was featured in many publications in the European Theater and at home, with the caption "Reunion in Garmisch."

❧

I met another Bob one day in March 1947 when I was up at the Kreutzek skiing with Karl. Since Karl was German, he couldn't come into the Kreutzekhaus for lunch, so we arranged to meet again afterward, and went in by myself. Tables were pretty much taken and I asked to join a chap sitting alone. He turned out to be Bob Two, who was down from Heidelberg. We had a good chat, but when he invited me to ski with him, I had to tell him I had a date with Karl. Since I was Red Cross, however, and there to promote satisfying times for American guys, I said, "Would you like to come to our house for dinner?" Of course he would; the guys always welcomed an invitation to a home setting. So I told him where it was and how to get there and I'd see him again about five thirty.

That was the beginning of a long, rather serious relationship. Bob was a handsome clean-cut type whom I was always proud to be with, especially when he wore his Bavarian hat and smoked his pipe. He would have looked great on a magazine cover. He was a bit older than the average GI having come to the ETO from a tour of duty with the Marines in the South Pacific. As a wire chief in communications for the military at Heidelberg headquarters, he could keep in touch with me by phone, even though personal calls had been *verboten* or curtailed to a large extent. He came to Garmisch every weekend he could get off, spending a lot of time out at our house during the spring.

On Easter Sunday that year, the third anniversary of our sailing for the ETO, Bob Two and Elsie and I went to sunrise service on the Kreutzek. This time we made the cable car on time, and the minister did too. In the afternoon at the club a group of seventeen Ukranian children brought in from Mittenwald, most of them about five years old, sang and danced in their Russian costumes. The guys just loved them. We had two MPs dressed as big rabbits giving out chocolate bunnies to everyone, and at four we had our regular "Bayrisher Hillbilly Floor Show." Oh yes, there was also Darcy's "frame-up" for photographs—a chap in lederhosen, captioned "Easter Parade, 1947, Bahnhofstrasse, Garmisch."

Bob Two was now coming from Heidelberg nearly every weekend, and we'd often take off on trips around the area. We didn't have to talk a lot of how we felt about each other. It was an understanding that grew out of our wish to be together and share the same kind of experiences. I was looking forward to a few days in Heidelberg about the middle of May. Bob had a special horse for me, with a planned program of riding, swimming, shopping, and clubbing. I'd never really seen Heidelberg, just driven through twice.

Late one Sunday night we had the living room to ourselves and had been lounging before a fire talking over the day. When it came time for Bob was to say goodnight and goodbye for the weekend, he stood up. After a pause he said, "I can't leave, Vi, without asking you this time—and the only way I can say it is—will you marry me?"

I can't say that I hadn't thought it might come to this, though I'd keep telling myself it would be a risky relationship. That night it was difficult to say "no," so I said, "Oh Bob, I don't know. We haven't known each other very long, and the war makes things look different than they really are," and other similarly lame excuses. I finally said, "Well, Bob, I promise I'll stay here in the ETO. I'll even take another assignment if need be, and we'll see what happens." When I said that I knew it answered another question I'd been pondering—about staying on or going home!

When spring skiing was pretty much gone in Garmisch, Elsie and I decided to go to Innsbruck for some Austrian shopping. I said, "You know, Elsie, I was in Innsbruck on July 3 back in '45 in a snow blizzard at the top of the mountain. There could still be good snow. Let's take our skis along so we can say we've skied in Austria."

Famous last words! I ended my skiing in Austria with a spiral fracture of the tibia and a fracture and splintering of the fibula just under the knee. That required a rescue-team ride off the mountain, an overnight in an Austrian hospital, an ambulance ride to Garmisch, and hospitalization there—but for only one night, since the break needed special care in Munich. With that kind of injury, had a plane been going to the States from Munich, I'd have been ZI'd: that is, sent to the Zone of the Interior—the States.

Bob hitchhiked or trained to Munich each weekend. I told him that had they insisted on the ZI, I'd have resigned from Red Cross to stay over. I even wrote my good friend Easton Rothwell in the State Department, who had his secretary type six original copies of a letter of recommendation that I could use in trying to find other employment in Germany if I left ARC. We even dreamed up the possibility of my spending the rest of my hospital stay in Heidelberg once I got a walking cast, but that idea was shattered when I got the second long leg cast and was transferred to Stuttgart. I had made many great friends during my hospital stay in Munich, and because I was a good patient, I was allowed to ride the ambulance to Garmisch for long weekend stays. Meanwhile, I transferred my directorship to Elsie.

There was a card from "The triumvirate" (Ed One, Ed Two, and Rafe), who'd been together at a ski resort in New Hampshire: "God we miss you! All we talked about were the events of last winter. Got in some good skiing, but the scenery at Franconia doesn't come close to Garmisch."

17 Going Home

About this time we had official word that the Olympic Club in Garmisch was to close as an American Red Cross operation. The army would take it over, and staff could sign on with them. It was hard to know that I wouldn't be going back, but I was lucky in one way: closing up the club fell to Elsie, with all the paperwork of army and Red Cross regulations. I recall her telling about the devil of time she had doing something with a water trailer that had been behind the club when we got there. Where it came from we never did know, but she had somehow to account for it on paper.

The girls had been great while I was away. At first they'd bring business questions to me in Munich or papers to sign, but as weeks went by, I delegated all this to Elsie. Harry sent up a huge portrait he'd done, plus some of his famous comic strips. There were notes from the Seethalers and the German staff.

During all the time Bob and I spent together, much of it just talking at my bedside, I found my earlier doubts coming back. Bob didn't necessarily want a clinging vine, but from things he said I gathered he felt less than my equal, in funny little ways but ways that seemed not the best foundation for a lasting intimate relationship—at least the way I wanted it.

At Stuttgart, I graduated from my long leg cast to a knee cast and finally to a walking cast. Because I'd done some typing for the doc and was such a good patient, he gave me a pass to go to Austria to see Elsie, who had transferred there from Garmisch. This was in August, five months after my accident! (Today it wouldn't take this long, but then I had to be hopitalized until they could send me back to duty.) I was about to get my cast off for good, but the doctor suggested

I'd better wait till I got back from the trip. Turned out great! I was special and babied, with others carrying my luggage.

Stuttgart, Germany, August 14, 1947
Though they told me I couldn't get into Austria, I got right through to Linz, near where Elsie is stationed. Her club's on an air base in an old barracks building that needs lots of work.

We got tickets for the world-famous Salzburg Music Festival. We attended an opera at the historic hall, but I'll remember longest being at the first postwar production of *Yederman* (Everyman) in the *dom* (cathedral) square. This had been a traditional annual performance until Hitler banned it because of its religious flavor.

I got a ride from Salzburg to Munich with some headquarters people I met there, and spent Monday taking stock. I found that sick leave was not cumulative; and one could have only twenty-four days in any one year. When that ran out, they'd started using up my annual leave, of which I had about forty-three days. Together with holidays, it carried me on a paid basis pretty much through July. That means I have no leave time left; any I take before leaving for home will have to be without pay. I talked by phone with Miriam Fay at general headquarters. She was great and said I could clear through Munich and then come on up to general headquarters, now in Bad Wildungen.

The next big news: I got my cast off when I got back. The leg doesn't look bad at all. It feels practically good as new, except for the swollen ankle. I'll have to work now to get that leg suntanned to go with the other one. I just may get to drive to Garmisch this weekend with a WAC lieutenant who has a car. I hope I can; one doesn't see many WACs over here.

The weekend before I went to Austria, Bob came up with a jeep and we "did" Stuttgart. He let me drive (I was still wearing the walking cast, but it was on my left leg). I was in civilian clothes, and we were stopped by MPs who

thought I was a DP or a German fraulein. They asked for
my driver's license, which of course I didn't have with me.
But when they asked Bob if I'd been accustomed to driving government vehicles, I spoke up: "I'm with American
Red Cross. I've driven jeeps and weapons carriers and
even command cars around the Continent for over three
years." They believed me and let us go. I was glad, because Bob wasn't supposed to have taken the jeep out of
Heidelberg and had already gotten one ticket for speeding
on the autobahn—and that's hard to do!

∿

After some hydro- and physiotherapy I was finally dis-
charged—not back to duty but to leave without pay. All the
fight I'd felt when first hospitalized, about getting another
kind of job over there if Red Cross tried to send me home,
had dissipated. I shared this feeling with Bob. There was no
big scene but a kind of mutual understanding that these past
five months had been special and almost a trial marriage. It
had given at least me enough time to sort out thoughts and
feelings. I saw him for the last time just before leaving for
headquarters to clear.

I had orders for a leave trip to Rome and stopped in Garmisch on the way. I was sorry I'd gone. I did see some of our
German staff, but our Olympic Club was again a local theater. This time the trip into Italy was legitimate and by train. I
sent home a postcard from Rome: "Two days in Florence and
four days here in Rome. It's fabulous. So crammed full of
history and religion it makes one's head swim! I'll soon be on
my way home!"

Once I was officially scheduled for return to the States, I had
a letter from Ed One of the old Garmisch skiing triumvirate.
He was at Yale and said to cable him when I was to arrive. If he
could, he'd try to meet me in New York City, and just maybe
even Ed Two could come down from Harvard and help me
celebrate my first night in New York. "What a time we could
have talking over all the old skiing days and parties at your
house!" Garmisch had captured the hearts of many.

My port of embarkation that September of 1947 was Bremerhaven, where I made inquiries and found out how to smuggle out the two automatics—the tiny 45 I'd received for the shooting in Ludwigslust, and the 32 they gave me in Berlin to protect myself if need be. I came home on the *General Black* one of the small Liberty ships—quite a comedown from the *Queen Mary*. We did get to sleep out on deck under the stars a couple of nights. My stomach seemed to behave better in the fresh air.

Those quiet hours with endless boundaries of water and sky lent themselves to thought and wonder. After three and a half years of an artificial world of war and occupation in foreign lands, with people of other countries—what would it be like to come back to everyday living in one's own small world? Though it would be good to see family and friends, the days that lay ahead didn't seem all that alluring.

Ed One had exams and couldn't come to New York, it turned out, but had made a reservation for me at a hotel in New Haven so I'd be sure to stop. Some of my ship compadres and I had a short time in the Big Apple and embarrassed ourselves at a restaurant one evening when we forgot and left cigarettes for a tip instead of cash! Shopping became mandatory; I found that while we'd been busy in the ETO, designers had decided to lengthen skirts.

Ed One showed me around Yale and stayed at the hotel with me in New Haven. Since Ed Two was back at Harvard Law School, I went up to touch base and compare notes with him and Darcy, who had an apartment in Cambridge. Pete was at the Wharton School of Business in Philadelphia and said he'd disown me if I didn't stop on the way home. I saw my first television there!

Finally I was back in my hometown. I'd called so many places "home" in those three and a half years that after the initial excitement of seeing family and friends and being a center of attention for a short time, coming back to Minnesota was a letdown. Even though I was asked to speak at the local Red Cross, the Rotary Club, and Teachers College, I kept remembering the letter Mary had written me when I was still in Garmisch: "Vi, you'll be amazed when you get home how little you have in common with people. I'm just now beginning to get my feet planted on the ground. And dates with fellows who weren't even in the Army are perfectly ghastly." And Elsie had written: "I've found it difficult to adjust to a civilian way of life. My girl friends are all married and raising families, and after the initial 'Ohs and ahs' we haven't much in common any more. I've admired more children than a governor running for reelection."

Several of us had difficulty deciding what kind of jobs we wanted or, if we knew, finding them. Smitty wrote suggesting resorts and said that Bill Kerr (who had managed the Kreutzekhaus in Garmisch) was manager at Sun Valley. But when I wrote Bill, he replied that most of his staff of seven hundred were college kids working for a pittance.

Then a letter came from the Midwestern Area Office of the American Red Cross. They'd reviewed my national personnel file and wanted me to consider a position in Services to Veterans Hospitals. I wasn't excited about staying with Red Cross, but not knowing what I truly wanted to do or where to begin, it was easiest to say "yes"—at least until something significant turned up. I accepted with the understanding that I be assigned to duty later that spring. I'd planned a trip to the West Coast to see Bob One and ARC and Reed friends in California and Oregon before I got involved with another job.

I was assigned as a staff assistant at the Veterans Administration Hospital in Dearborn, Michigan. After nine months of working with eight hundred women volunteers and planning programs with too many other volunteer organizations vying for time, I decided this wasn't for me. Besides, it resurrected old feelings about the artificial life I needed to shed in getting back to reality. We'd used cigarettes for legal tender. We'd arbitrarily taken over some of the best buildings, homes, and hotels in another country. I could officially travel and stop almost anywhere for free meals and lodging and be warmly welcomed by the military, if for no other reason than that I was an American woman. To some of the people there we were saviors; to others we were ugly Americans. And when I told my story to a chap who'd been in the South Pacific, he wrote back:

Your story verifies a long cherished belief: "the sonzabitches in Europe got all the wine, women and song and we got the dirty end of the stick!" Your story unintentionally reveals the stark contrast between life in Europe and life in, say, New Guinea, for servicemen. In all my time in the South Pacific I received one Coca-Cola from the Red Cross—this from a surly girl in a small tent near Buna, New Guinea. My God! Compare this to your account of European goodies, and the direction of the U.S. war effort is easy to figure out.

Nevertheless, staying in the ETO for the occupation had helped me make the transition; one knew the artificial life was about to be over and could propare to face the future, wherever it might lead. The VA hospital experience was also a small bridge that led to resolutions. At least I knew one thing I didn't want to do!

I now often think of the big loop I made, beginning in Oregon and ending in Minnesota, with so many zigs and zags across the Unites States and Europe. And today, how many years and wars later, I think of a larger world loop on which World War II stands out as a major stop for me.

Looking back, I'm not proud of some of the things I did. How could I walk into other people's homes and pick out furniture I liked and assumed they could do without? But I also look back and wonder how I handled all ranks of personalities and untold contingencies as well as I did. It was a graduate education with a major in humanities and minors in psychology, personnel, and business administration.

Even more important, there was that "something" that happened to us who were there—something personally and deeply significant we shared that's impossible to describe to anyone who hasn't experienced it. It's a pride, yes, but it has nothing to do with power or politics or patriotism. It's that secret sharing, that gift given to those of us who shared a war and came home—something we shall cherish the rest of our lives.

Epilogue

Just before the fortieth anniversary of D-Day an article in *Time* magazine (May 28, 1984) said:

The ceremonies in Normandy will celebrate the victory and mourn the dead. They will also mourn, almost subliminally, a certain moral clarity that has been lost, a sense of common purpose that has all but evaporated. Never again, perhaps, would the allies so handsomely collaborate. The invasion of Normandy was a thunderously heroic blow dealt to the evil empire. Never again it may be, would war seem so unimpeachably right, so necessary and just. Never again, perhaps, would American power and morality so perfectly coincide.

There *was* real purpose for us in World War II. Adolph Hitler gave us that. Since then, among how many questionable conflicts around the world, not one has provided that feeling of being "unimpeachably right." Worse still, we're beginning to question the "perfect coinciding of American power and morality." And although I read with pride the deeply positive feelings of the *Time* article, I have discovered with disillusionment some incidents even in *that* war of which we cannot be proud.

During the summer of 1983, while visiting near Plymouth on the southern coast of England, we saw a marble monument with the following inscription:

THIS MEMORIAL WAS PRESENTED
BY THE UNITED STATES ARMY AUTHORITIES
TO THE PEOPLE OF THE SOUTH HAMS WHO GENEROUSLY LEFT THEIR
HOMES AND THEIR LANDS TO PROVIDE A BATTLE PRACTICE AREA FOR
THE SUCCESSFUL ASSAULT ON NORMANDY IN JUNE 1944. THEIR ACTION
RESULTED IN THE SAVING OF MANY HUNDREDS OF LIVES AND CONTRIB-
UTED IN NO SMALL MEASURE TO THE SUCCESS OF THE OPERATION. THE

AREA INCLUDED THE VILLAGES OF BLACKAWATON, CHILLINGTON, EAST
ALLINGTON, SLAPTON, STOKKENHAM, STRETE AND TORCROSS, TOGETH-
ER WITH MANY OUTLYING FARMS AND HOUSES.
Plinth on Slapton Sands, Devon   Normandy Terrain

We had lunch at a pub that the Americans had frequented
during that time. The innkeeper called our attention to many
framed mementos above the hearth, which gave us the story
we had never been told. A friend from my WAAC days later
sent me an article from her Fargo-Moorehead newspaper
(Sunday, November 15, 1987) which spelled it out. It began,
speaking of this very innkeeper, "Thanks to the tireless 18-
year effort of an English innkeeper, the 749 forgotten American soldiers of World War II are about to be honored," and
went on:

It seems that the tragedy began on the night of April 27, 1944, when
30,000 untried men of Maj. Gen. Raymond O. Baton's 4th U.S. Infantry Division, the 279th Engineer Combat Battalion and the 70th
Tank Battalion staged a mock assault at Slapton Sands. The exercise, code-named Operation Tiger, was a dress rehearsal for the
Normandy invasion six weeks later. Everything went wrong.
     Several German patrol boats got in among the U.S. landing craft
and sank two of them. Panicky GIs opened fire on their own boats,
believing they were firing at the Germans. Others, unaware that
they had been given live ammunition, thought the explosions and
flames around them were part of the exercise. Men drowned and
their tanks and trucks sank. When dawn broke, hundreds of soldiers were found floating upside down in the cold channel water.
Improperly instructed, they had incorrectly placed their life vests
around their waists instead of under their arms.
     Operation Tiger resulted in one of the largest losses of American
lives in a single incident in the war. The death toll was more than
four times higher than the 179 GIs who would die on Utah beach.

Nor were these British civilians who gave up their homes
and our own military who lost their lives in "rehearsal" the
only ones who suffered at our hands in questionable ways.
Kurt "Harry" Walter, the German artist at our Olympic
Club in Garmisch, had been with the German signal corps in

Paris and surrendered to the Americans after D-Day. In a recent letter, he wrote of events that saw no publicity until many years later.

We English-speaking crew members on the late night shifts tuned in on Allied Forces radio in Europe. We believed in the prospects and promises transmitted over the networks, and were misled to say the least. I had to leave all my gear and personal belongings behind in the hotel room where U.S. soldiers picked me up. I was under the impression that I would have to get myself registered and then could go home, a mistake I should bitterly regret.

I never got back to my room, and all I had was the uniform I was wearing. We were headed for places like Ludwigshafen, which had 120,000 POWs, and Heilgronn with as many. About 5,000 of us were stuck in a stockade with one faucet (one!). Each man was entitled to one cup of water a day. Food was scarce, mortality high, and the whole thing was in ridiculous contrast to what we had listened to and believed in.

Nevertheless, and especially as a woman, I'm thankful to have been included by the military as a complementary part of the last "good war." For all of us it brought deep community and pride of country—something today's baby boomers and youth have not had the privilege to experience, as our country still suffers the aftermath of Vietnam and faces power challenges ahead.

I often think of what Tony Seethaler, my German club director, once said to me in Garmisch. "I wish, Miss Vi, that the powers that be would settle things and let us get on with our lives." I can only hope that as a world leader we can once again display not only the "rightness" the *Time* article mentioned but also the merging of "American power and morality," becoming a protector of the *peoples* of nations as we continue to be embroiled in conflict with their leaders.

After my VA stint with American Red Cross, I turned down an invitation from Elsie to come to Berkeley, because I didn't like big cities, and accepted another invitation from hometown friends in Santa Fe, New Mexico, to stay with them till I found a job and apartment. I loved the Southwest, but after spending six wonderful years working for an architect and as office manager at the Chamber of Commerce in Santa Fe, I decided once again I was in a comfortable rut. This time I accepted Elsie's invitation.

As I left Santa Fe in the late 1950s, had anyone told me I'd end up in the Unitarian ministry, I'd have said they were dreaming. Yet, through many serendipitous turnings, this is just what happened. Three years later I was the first woman to be graduated with a certificate of completion from Starr King School for the Ministry (Unitarian) after having been admitted to its graduate program, again without my undergraduate degree! I was then in my forties with no degrees. Some years later, the faculty at my theological school recommended to the Board of Trustees that I be granted my graduate degree retroactively to 1962. I now hold the Master of Divinity degree and have served Unitarian Universalist churches in Provincetown, Massachusetts, on the tip of Cape Cod; Calgary, Alberta, in the shadow of the Canadian Rockies; and Tallahassee, Florida, in the deep South. After retiring from my last church in Kent, Ohio, I joined a Red Cross friend in a new solar home in Vermont for a while before returning to Minnesota.

Though I never married, I feel I've had more significant relations with men than have most married women. It has had something to do, I feel, not with promiscuity but with a rare kind of intimacy—a relationship involving sufficient courage to share one's emotional and intellectual self to a point of vulnerability. Several men I knew in the ETO, all now married with families, are still part of a vast circle of friends across the United States and Canada. We understood and still understand each other. World War II veterans will know what I mean. The nation will celebrate during the fiftieth anniversary of that history-making war, but only those of us who were there can share in a kind of kindred "knowing," its deeper meanings, with a pride, but also a wonder about all the questionable conflicts which were to follow.